BEYOND THE CLASSROOM

Dorothy Elmhirst, one of the foundes of the Dartington Hall Trust.

BEYOND THE CLASSROOM

DARTINGTON'S EXPERIMENTS IN EDUCATION

MARK KIDEL

First published in 1990 by
Green Books
Ford House, Hartland
Bideford, Devon EX39 6EE

Typeset by Fine Line Publishing Services
Witney, Oxon.

Printed by Hartnolls
Victoria Square, Bodmin, Cornwall

British Library Cataloguing in Publication Data
Kidel, Mark
Dartington: experiments in education.
1. Devon, Dartington. Independent progressive schools
I. Title
371'. 04'09423592

ISBN 1-870098-19-6

Contents

Leonard Elmhirst, co-founder and later Chairman of Dartington Hall.

Three weeks ago I was spending the weekend at Dartington, and talked much with L. Elmhirst about his experiences with Tagore at Santiniketan and elsewhere. He himself has done wonderful things at Dartington, which is one of the few places in the world where one can feel an almost unqualified optimist.

Aldous Huxley, in a letter to Tagore's biographer, Krishna Kripalani, 1963.

PREFACE

T HIS BOOK was originally commissioned by the Dartington Hall Trustees, while I was employed by them as 'Interpretation Officer'. This unusual title — borrowed from the world of environmental education and the US National Parks — referred to a job which was, to say the least, open to interpretation. Central to the idea — as I interpreted it — was an attempt to understand the Dartington Hall Trust's work, both present-day and historical, in terms of the 'languages' or 'currencies of speech' as Maurice Ash put it, in use at Dartington. Recognising that the 'languages' we use to define and understand the contexts within which we live, do not just describe those realities but actually contribute towards shaping our perception, I became slowly aware of the need to clarify some of the accepted truths — often expressed in tired slogans — associated with Dartington's history.

The theme of 'Learning by Doing' was the focus of a special issue of *Dartington Voice* — the community publication, which I edited at the time — in which it became clear that Dartington had a very special role in defining and exploring a range of educational issues, not just the familiar progressive ideal of creating space for the individual child's or student's self-expression. This book attempts to develop this theme more fully, as I believe it is of relevance to all those concerned with education, in its widest sense.

Thanks are due to all those with whom I collaborated in one way or another at Dartington, including the many who may not to this day realise how much I learned from a very brief conversation. I would like, in particular, to thank John Lane, with whom I collaborated closely on many projects, and from whom I learned a great deal about how original ideas could be put into practice at Dartington; Pauline Vincent, for unstinting support in preparing the first typescripts of the book; Chris Zealley and Reginald Snell for their support and helpful editorial suggestions. I am particularly grateful to Maurice Ash, not only for his suppport, but also because his subtle and wise ideas contributed towards this book taking its particular shape and enabled my own understanding of Dartington and the world to mature as I wrote. Finally, I would like to thank Susan Rowe-Leete for much help and encouragement along the way, and for editing this book with great commitment and care.

THE DARTINGTON HALL TRUST

T HE DARTINGTON HALL TRUST has grown out of an experiment launched by Leonard and Dorothy Elmhirst, when they bought the run-down estate and dilapidated medieval hall in 1925, with a view to providing a focus for the revitalisation of the countryside. Their shared vision and Dorothy's wealth made possible a wide range of economic and cultural experiments whose influence has been felt in Britain and abroad. Leonard was particularly interested in farming, forestry and the need to revitalise rural areas, while Dorothy believed passionately in the potential of the arts as a channel for personal and social renewal. Dartington's longevity and current vitality owe a great deal to the founders' ability to create a flexible establishment which is surprisingly unfettered by rules or dogma.

The Dartington Hall Trust provides today a focus and support for a wide range of activities in the arts, education, farming, research and business. It is a unique organisation which has grown up gradually since 1925, through a series of projects based mainly around the medieval estate of Dartington Hall near Totnes in South Devon.

The Trust has a number of business investments, and 1,000 acres of agricultural land provide the basis for two share-farming operations. Education is, however, nowadays Dartington's main concern. The Dartington College of Arts is an independent college supported through the Polytechnics and Colleges Funding Council and provides courses in Art & Design, Music, and Theatre, with a stress on the central role of the arts in community life.

Dartington's other educational ventures include the Dartington Tech, which acts as an umbrella organisation for an expanding range of activities in the fields of youth training and continuing education. Other activities include the Devon Centre for Continuing Education, a short-course facility run by the Devon County Council, and the Adult Education Centre, which offers day and evening classes to local residents.

The College of Arts is the main sponsor of the Dartington International Summer School of Music, an International Dance Festival, and the Summer School of Art. The College is also closely involved in the promotion of a wide range of events, including exhibitions, theatre, concerts and films, most of which are organised or presented by Dartington Arts. Other annual events include the Dartington Conference, sponsored by the Dartington Hall Trust.

The experimental and enquiring nature of many Dartington activities is reflected in the work of the Dartington Social Research Unit, which studies deprivation and delinquency in children.

Following important educational projects in Yorkshire during the 1960s, Dartington has recently established two other Trusts, the Elmhirst and Ivanhoe Trusts, both of which are designed to help bring new life to communities in which mining has ceased to be a substantial source of employment.

Dartington's influence has spread into North Devon; in the setting up, twenty years ago, of a successful glass factory in Torrington; by the establishment of the Beaford Centre, a unique and pioneering venture providing cultural activities in a rural area; and most recently in the establishment of the Dartington North Devon Trust, with a role as a catalyst to economic and social development — offering a wide variety of youth and adult training programmes, activities for retired people, and services for those starting in business.

In 1988, the Trustees published a general statement about Dartington's 'Aims and Policies'. According to this document, the 'General Aim' of the Dartington Hall Trust is:

"To promote patterns of living which draw strength from a rural environment, are economically viable, meet the emerging needs of society and offer the individual a fulfilling, well-balanced life."

The Aims are more full described in the following four paragraphs:

"Dartington's endeavour has always been a response to human need; never has it been based purely on theory. The Trust views life as a whole. It seeks to bring together those elements which, in general, our society regards as separate and, indeed, opposed. The Trust strives to break down barriers, to make connections, to free the energy inherent in seemingly contradictory forces.

Dartington identifies the challenge of change with the necessity to discover fresh forms of integration.

Dartington was founded out of the vision of living and learning as one, and person and world as whole and holy. A concern for the arts as a channel for personal and social renewal is central to the commitment to education.

Dartington seeks to explore new ways of living which draw strength from a sense of place and that which is small-scale and personal."

June 1989

For further reading:
The Elmhirsts of Dartington by Michael Young, Routledge & Kegan Paul, London, 1982
Dartington by Mark Kidel, Webb & Bower, Exeter, 1982

INTRODUCTION

T HIS IS A BOOK about a neglected but very important aspect of progressive education. Ordinarily, the word 'progressive' conjures up images of individual freedom and an imaginative approach to learning, in contrast to the discipline and standardisation of traditional book-and-rote learning. There is, however, another stream of educational experiment, no less radical in its implications, although not as easily identifiable with the orthodoxies of liberalism or the political left.

When we speak of education, we refer, conventionally, to a process which involves a specialised activity that normally takes place within specific boundaries: a school or college. Here, children or students are removed from the everyday world to be taught, as this is believed to be the best way to facilitate learning. The idea that learning might be returned, as it were, to the world, by breaking down or at least softening the barriers between school and work, family and general community life, has always been — and still is — radical.

There is an important difference between a purely functional approach to vocational education (e.g. 'on the job training'), and the radical moves with which this book is mostly concerned. At Dartington, the barriers between the institution and the world were not just broken down, but this was done as a fundamental part of a unique effort at rebuilding community, at making the world whole again. It is in the context of reintegration, therefore, that we must look at Dartington's contribution to education, just as much as in terms of concerns for the needs of the individual child.

Education at Dartington has usually been exclusively associated with a style of schooling that centres on the needs of the individual child. While never as radical as Neill's Summerhill, Dartington Hall School was one of the pioneering progressive schools, exercising undoubted influence on the state system, particularly at the primary level. The (much-publicised) collapse of the School in the early 1980s strengthened this somewhat one-sided understanding of the 'Dartington approach' to education, for the media focused exclusively on a received image of Dartington-styled education. But, while child-centered schooling has always been a Dartington ideal, there have been other objectives, perhaps more implicit than explicit, which have never attracted the attention of newspapers hungry for scandal.

Alongside the undoubtedly progressive aspects of the venture launched by the founders of the Dartington Hall Trust, Leonard and Dorothy Elmhirst, in 1925, there was a less obviously newsworthy attempt at reconstructing a traditional country estate; a community of adults and children that would be animated by a programme of loosely interconnecting projects, and by the idealism of the founders and those drawn to them.

A central element of the Elmhirsts' vision — of a world re-constructed as one, with the specialisations of modern society brought together around a central defining form arising out of a sense of place — was the idea of 'learning *from* life' rather than *about* it: of 'learning by doing'. In such a community, learning would not be abstracted from the world, conducted within the walls of an institution, and divided into separate subjects. It would, as far as possible, be an integral part of everyday life, and arise naturally out of work and other essential communal activities.

The phrase 'learning by doing' conjures up a spirit of practical exploration, an adventurous attitude to change, and a willingness to test the validity of vision in the ground of the everyday world. As a general tendency towards experiment, the idea of learning by doing at Dartington has spread well beyond the narrow confines of what is normally labelled as education: the entire range of activities at Dartington has had, in the broadest sense, an

2

Introduction

educational basis and the Trust's central purpose can be seen as
one of education.

'Learning by doing' is not unique to Dartington: it is implicit in
the world-wide and ancient tradition of apprenticeship, the
factory schools of the 19th century, vocational training and
education, and more recent experiments in the USSR, China and
the Third World. More explicitly, it has provided one of the key
slogans for the progressive movement in 20th-century education,
as well as being central to the language and practice of contemporary youth training and work experience.

What then makes Dartington's practice of 'learning by doing'
so unusual? Firstly, there has been a unique commitment, which
stretches back over more than half a century, to a breakdown of
the usual barriers between classroom or lecture hall and the
world. This perspective has given rise to a remarkable range of
projects, from the brave de-schooling of the Estate's first five
years, through to the formal requirements of practice in a 'social
context' in the present-day College of Arts.

It is Dartington's wider purpose which distinguishes the
Trust's experience: 'learning by doing' has not only characterised
specific projects, but also the development of the whole Dartington Estate as a matrix for social, economic and cultural experiment. Experiment, learning, and education — both formal and
informal — are central to the whole scheme. Over the years, such
a purpose has been reflected in agricultural innovation, pioneering work in forestry, small-scale rural industries, the artificial
insemination of cattle, the development of a tourist centre based
on a disused 19th-century port and mine, and many other
examples of what might be called action research, quite apart
from Dartington's more clearly educational enterprises.

Dartington has always seen itself not only as a seedbed, but
also as a laboratory in which new ideas can be put to the test. The
Trust has always offered its experience as a model from which the
rest of the world can learn. Reflecting an unusually experimental
cast of mind, Leonard Elmhirst preferred to speak of 'positive or
negative results', rather than success or failure. Each new project
was approached as a venture into uncharted territory, whose
progress was intended to be rigorously monitored: the Dartington

3

venture was set up, in many ways, along the lines of a scientific experiment.

One of the central features of Dartington as a laboratory for social change, has been its ability to offer a measure of shelter from the contingencies of economics: to offer a space where social innovators can follow creative hunches. This unusual measure of independence has been directly related to the availability of financial resources, and in recent years the Trust has been less free to experiment: new ventures have increasingly had to rely on local or central government assistance.

The Trust's belief in experiment and its commitment to the process of trial and error have made it a unique institution — if such a term can be used to describe the loose but interconnected range of projects, departments and businesses that belong to the Dartington 'family'. Dartington's commitment to experiment creates a tension which makes life at Dartington both challenging and yet strangely unsettling. Many of those who work at Dartington, particularly at management level, speak of the way in which they have been stretched — and this can be a negative experience if the balance is tipped too far.

In the early days, the fact that learning was central to every project at Dartington was much more evident. The School was the Estate, and the Estate was the school, at least in theory. 'Seniors' and 'juniors' — as all adults and children on the Estate were respectively called — were supposed to share in a common learning process. Life on the Estate was to be an adventure for all. The intimacy of scale, the force of pioneering enthusiasm, and the charisma of the founders, undoubtedly created a remarkable context in which, for a few years, distinctions between learning and doing, school and life were blurred almost into non-existence.

In later years, projects proliferated: the Elmhirsts' many enthusiasms and their willingness to delegate led to a drift away from the centre, and departmental boundaries and separate group interests rapidly emerged. There is no doubt that Dartington experienced a retreat from radical experiment in the early 1930s and that this change reflected a gradual entrenchment of established interests. The establishment of a separate school, with a strong and independently-minded headmaster, suggests a

4

partial loss of faith in the vision of integration which had so powerfully inspired the first five years. 'Learning by doing' may have remained one of the educational principles behind the new school's progressive style and curriculum, but it came increasingly to be seen in terms of the School's *internal* educational programme rather than in relation to the Estate as a whole.

The Estate, with its wide-ranging mix of activities, may have finally succumbed to the specialist boundaries that exist in the world at large, but the original integrating impulse nevertheless left its mark. The Dartington experiment may not originally have had a set of clear goals, or 'Benedictine Rules' — a fact that Leonard Elmhirst emphasized very strongly at a meeting in the early 1970s — but there have always been echoes of the founding mythology. The Estate's almost dream-like beauty has never failed to conjure up the possibililty of a restored Eden: a community in which the warp and weft of social life provide shelter and a sense of identity to its inhabitants. It is perhaps ironic that this vision works most powerfully for outsiders and newcomers; the reality of everyday existence on the Estate is inevitably less romantic.

The dream, however, is a strong and enduring one, and it has continued to fill the imagination of those drawn to Dartington. The promise of an integrated community in which boundaries between different aspects of life are broken down, is a deeply attractive one, and it is in this context that we should look at Dartington's various attempts at drawing together 'learning' and the world beyond school or college walls.

Dartington's experience is important too for the world outside the Hall and Estate; for the ideals which the place and its history conjure up belong to a collective dream, a vision which is bound to haunt all societies whose development has necessitated specialisation and fragmentation. At Dartington the dream has in various ways been put to the test. Such an experiment is quite unique, and merits reflection.

Work experience at Dartington.

CHAPTER ONE

'Learning by Doing'

THE IDEA IN EDUCATIONAL HISTORY

"BUT ALL LEARNING is by doing!", a Dartington Hall School teacher once exclaimed to me in frustration, when I was preparing an issue of *Dartington Voice* based on that theme. He added that essay-writing, arithmetic, and the study of geography all involved a certain 'doing', although he accepted that its character varied according to the subject.

This teacher was, in his own terms, quite right, for even thinking or imagining can be defined as varieties of doing. The use of the phrase 'learning by doing' in the context of this book, however, is both more and less precise. Firstly, it describes specific activities in which the learner is directly involved in a project which approximates or belongs to the 'real' world beyond the specialist place of learning: a school farm or pottery training workshop, for instance. But 'learning by doing' is also used as a phrase which describes a general tendency towards learning *from* life rather than *about* it. It represents a preference for first-hand experience of 'being' and 'doing' in the world rather than accumulating second- or third-hand information about it. It can, perhaps, be described as a *process* -rather than *product* -orientated way of learning or acquiring skills; or to use Erich Fromm's terms, as more concerned with *being* than *having*.

The looseness of the phrase 'learning by doing' is inescapable, but this in itself may be useful, for it forces us to reflect upon what we understand by the term 'education' and to question some of our assumptions and prejudices. The idea of 'learning by doing' represents, above all, a reaction against the

7

primacy or over-valuing of another kind of learning: the acquisition of academic skills and factual knowledge from books. There is, as well, an almost instinctive dissatisfaction with the isolation of school and college from other areas of life, the tyranny of subjects, and the over-specialisation of the teaching profession.

In reaction to our culture's relentless progress towards an increasingly academic and specialised schooling, we have become fascinated by images of pre-industrial communities in which institutional education plays no part. Such a reaction is tinged with nostalgia, but this is not an entirely gratuitous feeling, for it is intimately tied up with a fundamental desire for inter-relatedness and stability.

This backward or sideways glance at other cultures arises out of a genuine unease with the convention of an education which 'leads out' rather than initiating or gathering in, (from the latin *educare*, which is related to *e-ducere*, to lead from).

In traditional societies, children gradually emerge into the world of adulthood, learning complex manual skills alongside their elders, and being initiated into the culture and mysteries of the group. Learning in such a context involves acquisition of basic skills, language, the means for physical survival, and perhaps a specific craft. Every aspect of learning is directly related to the growing child's immediate surroundings. The myths, stories, codes of conduct and religion of the group are passed on orally through rituals and initiation ceremonies, or other designated rites of passage. This kind of learning process involves developing a sense of identity within a social group and geographical place, and the integration of the child into the group. In the context of a culture which places a high value on stability, each person has to be 'fitted' into an unchanging tradition. Through in some sense being made complete, each member of the group becomes one with it. But completeness here is not seen (as it might be in our progress- and goal-driven culture) as growth or the maximisation of potential: such wholeness suggests instead a coming into social being, an awakening to a role circumscribed and given meaning by a traditional framework of time and place.

Some aspects of this world-view still inform our own culture and some seem to reflect universal patterns and concerns, but the discontinuity and re-structuring that have resulted from the growth of cities, industrialisation and the accompanying break-down of small and relatively static communities, make for a much more fragmented and complex picture, in which progress is valued at the expense of continuity and tradition.

However, the process of learning and the business of education were not just affected by the rise of a city-based industrial society. Alongside this process, and intimately related to it, there emerged a world-view which has radically altered our relationship to the world around us, our ideas about nature, history and truth. The scientific revolution and the cult of objective factual knowledge have necessitated a fundamentally different approach to the raising of children, and their preparation for the adult world.

Learning has evolved from the practical handing on of knowledge skills from one generation to the next, into a process of acquiring abstracted knowledge about the world with a view to mastering its complexities: to measure, quantify, categorise, and eventually predict and control. A 'man of learning' was known for his detachment, and the 'learning' cultivated during the Enlightenment and the scientific revolution has profoundly influenced our subsequent understanding of education. From the 18th century onwards 'learning' became increasingly understood as being exploratory and liberating: a move away from darkness into light, from ignorance to knowledge.

Knowledge, after the Enlightenment, was seen in material and outer terms; the value of such knowledge, it was believed, derived from the mind's ability to detach itself from the flow of events around it and to abstract knowledge from experience. Such knowledge — the domain of the mind rather than of the heart or body — is a kind of commodity which can be accumulated, expanded, improved and revised through the passage of time: knowledge has frontiers, which it is the human mind's destiny to continuously expand.

In cultures which place a value on tradition rather than progress, knowledge works instead as a kind of container: it offers security and continuity and is closely bound up with a group and personal experience of identity, place and meaning. It cannot be improved; only strengthened through ritual remembrance, the oral repetition of story and myth, and the cyclical patterns of each year. The strength of this kind of knowledge derives from its capacity to hold together: to provide boundaries which represent a recognition of the value and mystery of an 'un-known' that cannot be conquered by the mind, only hinted at through myth.

Education — while retaining some of the traditional notion of programming, training, or initiating a child for participation in a specific adult social group — acquired, after the 18th century, another parallel meaning connected with its enlightening or freeing aspect. The progressive movement in education, with its roots in the 18th century, has always emphasised the liberating qualities of knowledge, thus inevitably understating education's traditional roles as a means of integrating and initiating.

The liberal or radical impulse which runs through the progressive movement and fired much of the Dartington experiment is, therefore, inherently de-stabilising; it encourages questioning, exploration and an open attitude towards change. It is, in an essential way, at odds with the slowness, predictability, repetition, and cyclical character of tradition. According to the liberal cast of mind, 'learning' represents a movement outwards: an identification with the upward movement of the march of progress.

The conflict is central to the radical tradition in education. The idea of knowledge as an agent which frees humanity from the bondage of nature and provides the basis for political freedom, social mobility and scientific progress, minimises the need for containment and stability. For the progressive libertarian, containment equals constraint; for the individual spirit requires unbounded space in order to flourish.

Given the narrowly academic nature of much institutional learning in the 19th century, the authoritarian style of classroom and school and the political ends served by providing an educational pattern that passed on accepted knowledge, it is not surprising that radical and reformist movements should have advocated a more practical education, the study of public affairs rather than the classics, and a style of schooling that provided a blueprint for a better society.

Many educational experiments of the 19th and early-20th centuries understood the need for schools to provide more than a facility for the force-feeding of knowledge. In encouraging the idea of self-government within the school, some establishments provided a practical context in which children were expected to learn through experience the values of democracy, co-operation and compromise. This was a form of 'learning by doing' — and a similar approach has always been central to the philosophy and practice of Dartington Hall School. Such an approach was designed to make better citizens who might play an active part in bringing society closer to Utopia, rather than preparing children for a citizenship characterised by conformity to existing rules and conditions. The progressives have usually trusted in child-centered freedom rather than the use of authority and hierarchy. But such an approach, while liberating to the child, is out of tune with the discipline and constraints of a pre-industrial existence: the simple and basic rural life to which many progressives have been drawn.

The radicalism of the 19th and 20th centuries has suffered from being entangled with both Romanticism and the Enlightenment. There is within radicalism a pull backwards as well as forwards: in the direction of a restored golden age, as well as of a future Utopia. The issues of freedom and discipline have never been resolved and are, indeed, often avoided. These issues are central to the practice of 'learning by doing'. This uncomfortable issue has dogged many of the educational experiments at Dartington, and is indeed related to more general inherent contradictions in Dartington's definition of itself: an uneasy mix of optimistic but restless exploration and an equally forceful desire to restore a stable rural community, strengthened by forms that change slowly if at all.

THE DARTINGTON EXPERIMENT did not happen in a cultural vacuum. When Leonard and Dorothy Elmhirst bought the Dartington Estate in 1925, with the intention of setting up a 'school for adventure', they were not being quite as original and adventurous as the myths that emerged later would have us believe. The Elmhirsts were taking much of their inspiration from ideas which had been central to progressive education for many years. The typical 'new school' had been defined in an international newsletter published in the early 1920s as "a self-governing country boarding school in which all education is based on personal interest and experience, and intellectual work combined with manual activities in workshop and fields". In many respects, the Elmhirsts provided just such a school.

The most clearly visible sources of inspiration for Leonard and Dorothy were John Dewey and Rabindranath Tagore. But the wish to bring together School and Estate into an integral community also echoed many 19th-century experiments, as well as reflecting ideas put forward by Rousseau, Pestalozzi, Froebel, and other educational reformers. The progressive movement in education owes much to Jean-Jacques Rousseau, whose widely-read *Emile* was published in Britain in 1782. Rousseau was the first educational writer to place a central emphasis on the child. This focus was intimately related to Rousseau's belief in a 'natural man' and an original state of goodness and nature, which most societies had destroyed. The cult of the child and the trust in his or her ability to make the right choices provides the most consistent theme running through educational experiments of the 19th and 20th centuries. An education which preserved the qualities of children in their natural state would, it was agreed by reformers, ensure a just and free society. In Rousseau's conception education was, in the most fundamental sense of the word, political.

Along with stressing the value of children as persons in their own right, Rousseau emphasised the need to respond to children's natural enjoyment of manual work, as well as their interest in nature. *Emile*, the model child that Rousseau wrote about, "must work like a peasant and think like a philosopher." The idea that hands as well as heads should be used as part of learning was to become central to all those who were later inspired by Rousseau's radical pleas.

For Emile, experimental familiarity with the world of 'things' should precede intellectual and moral education, for manual work came closest to the state of nature. According to Rousseau and those who later echoed his ideas, there was a sense in which closeness to nature, and preferably a direct working involvement within it, enabled the child to avoid being corrupted by an 'un-natural' society. This rediscovery of nature (a 'going back to nature') lay at the heart of Romanticism and reflected a gut reaction to the 'artifice' of society, the materialist bias of science, and the growing inferno of the city and its industries.

Dartington, as an attempt to revitalize the countryside, represents a manifestation of the same tradition: a tradition that survives today in the ecological movement, and the continuing trickle of disillusioned city dwellers 'back' into the countryside. It is as if the memory or image of a more integrated and natural life has always haunted factory and city: an 'inner' demand for a society which reflects a sense of wholeness, and a reaction to the inevitable alienation of industrial work and urban anonymity.

Various themes emerge in the history of progressive education in the 18th, 19th and 20th centuries: the intrinsic value of the natural child, the importance of manual work as a balance to the intellect and as a means of being closer to nature, and a curriculum in tune with the demands of the world. Experiments reflected a combination of political radicalism, utilitarianism and puritanism, with work sometimes seen as a means of expiating original sin. Most of the ventures that emphasized the practical development of manual skills were designed for working-class children although the Quaker schools provide a notable exception.

The idea of the dignity of manual labour was central to many of these endeavours, and the combination of academic and manual work was seen as appropriate for the children of the working or agricultural classes. In the case of some — like Robert Owen's New Lanark Mill School, which integrated factory and school — one of the main objects was to develop the children's innate rationality and to prepare them for making a useful contribution to society. In others, the less radical aim was merely to provide an education fitting the child's social position, and facilitating his or her integration into work and society.

The notion of making school-work more relevant to the needs of the world beyond the institution's walls was common to all

13

progressive 19th-century educational experiments, including those designed for middle-class children. Classics gave way to the study of economics and society, and books were increasingly replaced by 'objects' and visits outside the classroom. In many cases children were expected to look after school gardens, household accounts, or take part in the school's 'Court of Justice', or in rudimentary forms of self-government.

Even before Rousseau's ideas had become widely known, William Gilpin had created what might be seen as a paradigm for later experiments in learning by doing. At the Cheam School, Gilpin attempted to move beyond the classical education of the public schools, and to reproduce in microcosm certain aspects of the outside world. The School was like a small state, and the boys were encouraged to keep small shops: "in which trade was done in gingerbread, cakes and apples." The children also kept small garden plots, although these were designed to introduce the idea of economics, rather than gardening.

The work of educational pioneers such as Pestalozzi, and Froebel left its mark on the thinking of practical innovators. Pestalozzi's emphasis on the child's senses and natural abilities, and Froebel's insistence on the child's self-discovery through play and exploration reinforced the child-centered bias that had grown out of Rousseau's ideas. Froebel's ideas, in particular, are central to the idea of the child 'learning by doing', rather than being somehow filled with a package of pre-digested knowledge. Froebel believed that children should find out what was right for themselves, rather than being told. This emphasis on knowledge from experience is central to many aspects of educational experiment at Dartington, whether in terms of working in farm, garden or workshop, or in terms of learning to live co-operatively in a self-governing community.

While it is important to place Dartington's emphasis on learning by doing within the broad context of educational experimentation in the 19th and early 20th centuries, there is a particularly strong connection with a stream of English progressive education that is rooted in the late Victorian 'counter-culture' which developed around the ideas of radicals like Ruskin, William Morris, Walt Whitman, Tolstoy, Edward Carpenter and

Patrick Geddes. The British expression of this movement focused mainly around the Fellowship of the New Life and its offshoot, the Fabian Society. It found practical expression in the Arts and Crafts Movement, the creation of the garden cities, and schools like Abbotsholme, Bedales and St. Christopher's.

The Fellowship and its idealistic sympathisers believed in no less than the radical re-structuring of society: it was, as W.A.C. Stewart writes, "a movement devoted to purifying cupidity in society by the labours of reformed and redeemed individuals, who through a self-supporting life based on manual work in communities, through education and religious communion and steadfast attention to social change, could reconstruct society". (*The Educational Innovators* Vol. 2, London, 1968). A return to more 'natural' living was essential to this new vision, as was a spiritual approach to manual work and the crafts.

In the prospectus for Abbotsholme — the first establishment to grow directly out of the Fellowship — Cecil Reddie, as founder and first head, wrote that the school was to "train [the boy] how to live." Such a training was only partly academic and a strong emphasis was placed on manual labour: the boys were to be taught carpentry, carving and metalwork, as well as the rudiments of agriculture and gardening.

Letchworth, the garden city, provided the ground for an experiment that in many ways foreshadowed Dartington's continuing idea of the Estate as classroom. The Garden City Theosophical School, which later became St. Christopher's School, drew much of its inspiration from the ideas of the Fellowship of the New Life; as it did from theosophy, one of the main spiritual streams of the 'counter-cultural' movement at the turn and beginning of the century. The Theosophical Educational Trust, upon which St. Christopher's was founded, set up in Letchworth a number of small enterprises which were designed to offer the boys and girls at the school first-hand experience of the world of work and business, as well as practical craftwork skills. The range of subjects included printing, tailoring, weaving, poultry-rearing, fruit-farming, a gardening shop and a 'pure food' factory. Only the printing business established itself properly, but before too long the enterprise found it difficult to combine its educational role with commercial necessities. The same problem was to play a major part in forcing the Elmhirsts to abandon the notion of children learning through participation in the various departments of the Dartington Estate, and the same difficulty arose again much more recently in the Dartington Pottery Training Workshop, which attempted to combine education with viability in the market-place.

What distinguished Dartington's heritage from the mainstream of the British progressive movement was the Elmhirsts' connections with America and India. Dorothy Elmhirst brought an enthusiastic commitment to the ideas of John Dewey. Her three children had attended Lincoln School in New York, which attempted to put Dewey's ideas into practice. Dorothy had also attended the influential educationalist's lectures in New York. The mark of Dewey's ideas was evident in the first Dartington School prospectus, and it was two disciples of Dewey's, Dr. A.T. Bonser and his wife, who were invited to make a first report on the School's progress in 1928.

Dewey's contribution to progressive American education at the turn of the century was considerable, and there is no doubt that his writings and the practical projects inspired by them had an important influence on the radical reforming circles to which Dorothy belonged. Dewey's contribution to education fits into a tradition that goes back to Rousseau via Froebel and Pestalozzi. He placed great trust in the child's innate abilities, and favoured a child-centered approach to identifying the child's particular needs, as well as maximising contact with the world. "Children", according to Dewey, "should learn by experiencing and doing." The idea of 'learning by doing' was particularly important to Dewey because it led the child outwards and actively into the world. In conventional education the child was passive, and was expected to take in the teacher's or textbook's version of reality. For Dewey, the teacher and curriculum must facilitate, before all else, the child's exploration of the world.

The ideal means for combining education and "growing up into the world" was, Dewey argued, "training through occupations"; by 'occupation', he meant "any continuous activity having a purpose". "Education through occupations", Dewey wrote, "combines within itself more of the factors conducive to learning than any other method. It calls instincts and habits into play: it is a foil to passive receptivity. It has an end in view; results are to be accomplished. Hence it appeals to thought." These 'occupations' included basic household and craft activities, but not just for their own sake: "we must conceive of work in wood and metal, of weaving and sewing, and looking at methods of living and learning, not as distinct studies. We must conceive of them in their social significance, as types of the processes by which society keeps itself going, as agencies for bringing home to the child some of the primal necessities of communal life".

Vocational subjects, for Dewey, were not to be taught as utilitarian skills but as "experiential points of departure for increasingly intellectualised ventures into the meaning of industrial society". The school was to be "an embryonic community life, active with types of occupation that reflect the life of the larger society" — in short, a microcosm of society.

For Dewey, the 'doing' behind 'learning' was never to be isolated from a sense of the whole: a sense of relationship between people, and with society.

Dewey was — in a pragmatic sense — an empiricist, in that he believed knowledge should be acquired through experience rather than received as 'lesson' or dogma. He was, however, uncomfortable with the dualistic tradition of philosophical empiricism, which was based on the separation of a knowing 'mind' from its object, 'matter'. He stressed the need to concretise knowledge, by relating it through 'doing' and experience to the world. Dewey was also concerned to break down the conventional and dualistic opposition between work and leisure, work and play, man and nature, thought and action.

Dewey hoped that such a reconciliation of opposites might change the nature of work and consequently the cast of society. The school was not just to reproduce a conventional "form of social life", but was intended to provide a model for the ideal society. Learning by doing, with Dewey, as with many other educational reformers, was not seen as a means of apprenticing or initiating children to the existing world around them, but as part of a scheme to change that world through an educational process that fulfilled the child's potential for self-regulation, exploration and co-operative participation in community.

There is a not entirely surprising parallel between Dewey and the Bengali poet and philosopher, Rabindranath Tagore (the other major direct influence on the Elmhirsts' venture at Dartington), for Dewey harked back to the integration of agrarian societies: societies in which each growing child learned to share in 'meaningful' work, understanding each stage of every 'making' process around her or him. The idea of 'meaning' was essential to Dewey, and inseparable from experience lived in the context of a community. In the ideal integrated community, individuals would be able to experience 'full lives', enriched by a sense of meaning that had been torn apart through the divisions and speciliasations of industrial society. Dewey applied some of these ideas to the Laboratory School which he set up in Chicago in 1896. Manual skills provided the first stage in a process which broadened out with the study of history, geography and later more abstract intellectual skills. Dewey's influence was perhaps strongest and most extended in the Gary (Indiana) schools' experiment before the First World War, which in the words of a contributor to *New Republic* — the radical weekly set up with Dorothy Elmhirst's financial backing — exemplified "the educational truth that learning can only come through doing."

The Gary schools went further, in many ways, than our so-called 'community colleges' do today: they were open twelve months of the year, and to all age groups. Each school within the system was organised as a miniature community. The school workshops handled the maintenance of buildings and equipment; the domestic science laboratories serviced the cafeteria; and the commercial science laboratories handled school records.

The idea of the school as microcosm of society was also central to Daddy George's Junior Republic, a school for juvenile delinquents that Leonard Elmhirst visited while he was at Cornell. The school included its own legislature and prison, and the children were fed in return for working in the school bakery, printing works, or hotel. Leonard also visited Homer Lane's Little Commonwealth, a similar venture in Britain and based on Lord Sandwich's estate. But the most important direct influence on

18

Leonard Elmhirst at this time — considering his years of personal involvement — was Tagore. Leonard worked with Tagore in Bengal from 1921 to 1924, establishing a number of parallel projects to revitalise the villages near Tagore's school at Santiniketan.

Tagore was a formidable figure, and greatly respected in his day. The influence this 'guru' must have exerted on a young and idealistic Englishman such as Leonard Elmhirst cannot be over-estimated — particularly one so disillusioned with his own society's conventions in education and religion. For Tagore, a revolution in education was necessary, for he passionately believed that conventional learning methods and the institutions that embodied them were in some essential sense opposed to the flow of life, and therefore were, inescapably, de-spiritualising. While Dewey provided a rationale for bringing learning and life together in secular and social terms, Tagore believed that education should take place in close relationship to nature (understood as an expression of the divine rather than the object of detached study) and involve, above all, the cultivation of the spirit.

As with many other educational reformers, including Leonard Elmhirst, Tagore reacted against his own unhappy schooldays: "In the usual course", he later wrote, "I was sent to School, but possibly my suffering was unusual, greater than that of most other children. The non-civilized in me was sensitive: it had a great thirst for colour, for music, for the movement of life. Our city-built education took no heed of that living fact. It had its luggage van waiting for branded bales of marketable result. The relative proportion of the un-civilized and civilized in man should be in the proportion of water and land on our globe, the former predominating. But the school had for its object a continual reclamation of the non-civilized. Such a drain of the fluid element causes an aridity which may not be considered deplorable under city conditions. But my nature never got accustomed to those conditions, to the callow decency of the pavement".

The price of an urban and industrial civilization removed from direct contact with the earth, nature and activities concerned with basic material survival, was a kind of drying-out: an estrangement from the experience of feeling and from life's flowing quality. Education, according to Tagore, needed to be locally-rooted and not transplanted into the hot-house of schooling. Tagore taught his own children at home and set up his first school at Santiniketan in 1901, the Bramacharya Asrama. "The life in the asrama", writes Krishna Kripalani, Tagore's biographer, "was simple to the point of austerity, the children had to attend to all their needs themselves which involved not a little manual labour".

Education was central to the rural reconstruction programme which Leonard Elmhirst took on for Tagore in the early twenties. But reconstruction was never conceived just in terms of economic development: the process was a qualitative rather than quantitative one, and the reconstruction was as spiritual as it was material. Part of Leonard's work involved preparing the ground for the Siksha-Satra, a weekly boarding school at Sriniketan. The Englishman brought with him the practical bias of Baden Powell and the Scout movement, with its emphasis on neighbourliness and service. "The sense of being in touch with life", as Leonard wrote a few years later, was one of the School's main features. The children "carried out a variety of duties, in dormitory, kitchen, garden, poultry-run and dairy. They learned games, songs and plays, carpentry and some other craft, and their games and writing were focussed on their daily experience." At Siksha-Satra, Tagore and Leonard Elmhirst set up the original model for what Gandhi later called 'basic education'; the Mahatma even borrowed staff from Tagore's Bengal boarding school when establishing his own educational projects.

Central to Tagore's philosophy and the projects in which Leonard Elmhirst assisted him, were manual labour, the development of basic household, garden and craft skills, and learning from life in the adult world rather than in an institution removed from the realities of life. The rationale for 'learning by doing', as an essential prelude to any kind of intellectual life, was multifaceted but originated — as it did for Rousseau, Dewey and other reformers — in a deep and instinctive reaction against excessive abstraction, specialisation, and that 'dried-out' absence of feeling and imagination which, in the eyes of some, characterised civilised urban life. For Tagore, 'learning by doing' engaged the body, and therefore the whole person; it also enabled the child to grow in close relationship to nature, learning to work with the land. Overcoming the divorce between learning and life opened the way for the reintegration of the inner and outer person. Such a rediscovery of the whole person was made possible through connecting the individual to his or her surroundings and fellow human beings. The reintegration of the person provided a core for the reconstruction of a living community, a shared existence which derived much of its meaning from place. In basing the Dartington experiment upon a real country estate, a place filled with atmosphere and history, the Elmhirsts were following in Tagore's footsteps and there is no doubt that Leonard himself drew much inspiration from the rural projects that he had helped establish in Bengal.

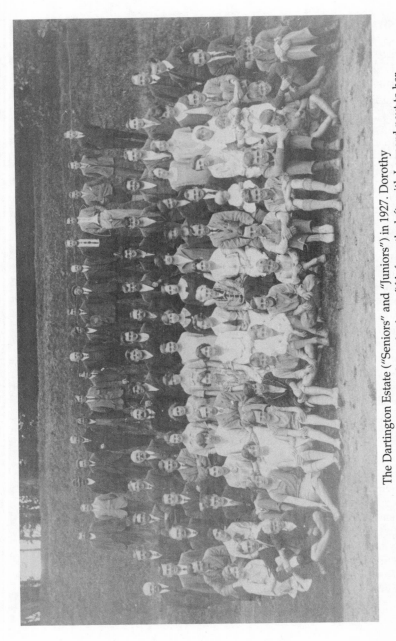

The Dartington Estate ("Seniors" and "Juniors") in 1927. Dorothy Elmhirst is seated in the second row from the front, fifth from the left, with Leonard next to her.

CHAPTER TWO

The School Without Walls

INITIAL EDUCATIONAL EXPERIMENTS
ON THE DARTINGTON ESTATE 1925–30

Your main object (at this stage) should be to keep out of your scholar's way all idea of such social relations as he cannot understand, but when the development of knowledge compels you to show him the mutual dependence of mankind, instead of showing him its moral side, turn all his attention at first towards industry and the mechanical arts which make men useful to one another. While you take him from one workshop to another, let him try his hand at every trade you show him, and do not let him leave till he has thoroughly learnt why everything is done, or at least everything that has attracted his attention. With this aim you should take a share in his work and set him an example. Be yourself an apprentice so that he may become a master; you may expect him to learn more in one hour's work than he would retain after a whole day's explanation.

> Jean-Jacques Rousseau, From *Emile*, quoted in C. H. Dobinson, *Jean-Jacques Rousseau: His Thought and Relevance Today* (London, 1969).

Is it not possible then to give freedom to the children to try out their own experiment and to build out of the experiment something of permanent value in the very field where we need end-less experiments of all kinds? But neither school nor ultimate community can afford to be in water-tight compartments and so each must grow as a vital part of the world around them, the rural or village life in that neighbourhood where they have set up their shrine to nature... What I mean to imply is this: that the time has come for the starting of innumerable small experiments in order to explore the great and unknown region of 'society' (where people are friends) and the possibilities of 'society' whose basis is personality (one of the products of friendship) and out of whose walls the City of Jerusalem will have to be built ... I don't think it matters in the least how small such experiments are, I should suspect them the moment they become too large, or to spread their religion in an organised way, because then the reign of personality is endangered, but that they should be innumerable and never of the same pattern, being built by people and not on paper from rules ...

I can see no reason why in some experiment where the children were encouraged to experiment for themselves how most easily to satisfy all their bodily needs in co-operation and to launch out into all the other fields of creation as well, if at the same time self-supporting craft industry and agriculture was carried on as part of the attempt of the school to relate education and life, and if the discoveries of such attempts at self-sufficiency and self-expression were also made easily available through children of the neighbourhood to the people of the locality, well at least it would be a worthwhile enterprise even if little were accomplished ... an atmosphere of service and self-sacrifice might from a tender seed eventually bud and blossom.

> Dorothy Elmhirst, in a letter to Professor Lindeman
> (7 January, 1925)

Leonard and Dorothy Elmhirst's initial educational experiment at Dartington between 1925 and 1930 represents one of the most radical attempts this century at breaking down the boundaries between learning and life. When the Elmhirsts bought Dartington Hall Estate with its partly ruined medieval buildings, the creation of a school was one of their foremost priorities. To call the project a 'school', or even to present it as distinct from the rest of the Elmhirsts' activities at Dartington, falls very short of accurately describing the venture. It is, however, difficult today (and it must have been equally, if not more difficult in the 1920s) to conceive of the project in any other terms, because the accepted definition of schooling is inextricably bound to the idea of a specialised and isolated process which 'qualifies', in a formal sense, for adult occupations and professions.

Whereas earlier progressive schools had built their own workshops and cultivated their own gardens, these were unequivocally 'school' facilities. Experiments like Daddy George's Junior Republic in the USA were set up as microcosms: models of the everyday world. At Dartington, however, Estate and School were in Dorothy's words to be 'married'; Estate life was to provide a natural rather than an artificial setting for facilitating the process of 'growing up'. Adults and children were not to be 'teachers' and 'pupils', but 'seniors' and 'juniors' — terms which referred to all those involved on the Estate, including gardeners and the other Estate workers. According to the Elmhirsts' original vision, the Estate, which in their view incorporated the School, was to provide the ground for the reconstruction of a small-scale rural community, an alternative to the dominant model of urban industrial life.

There is also a strong suggestion from the Elmhirsts' correspondence and writing between 1924 and 1926, that the children would, if left as much as possible to their own devices, choose for themselves a natural way of learning and living; it was almost as if the 'seniors' might learn from following the instinctive lead of the 'juniors', and rediscover with them a lost state of nature or wholeness. The radically experimental nature of the Elmhirsts' early vision for Dartington — with its faith in the child — suggests an unusual combination of idealism and bravery. It was moved as well by an almost child-like enthusiasm for risk and exploration. When the first School prospectus announced in its opening words, that "this school is for adventure", there was a sense in which the adventure was to be shared by 'juniors' and 'seniors', as joint pioneers of a new form of community life. Not just the School, but the whole Dartington project, was understood in terms of 'education' or 'learning' (defined in the broadest sense): all the departments were initially to provide a testing-ground for new ideas in agriculture, forestry, craft and other aspects of rural development, as well as, eventually, paying for themselves.

There was clearly, from the start, a certain ambivalence about the idea of having a 'school' at all; Leonard's own schooldays had been miserable, and he wrote to Wyatt Rawson, a former fellow undergraduate at Cambridge who was soon to be involved at Dartington: "I want the thing to grow quite naturally out of our own home life and never to mention the word school from the start" (Letter to W.R., 8th February, 1925, quoted in Michael Young's *The Elmhirsts of Dartington*). The 'School' was indeed to grow out of home life, as three of the first ten pupils were Dorothy's children by her marriage to Willard Straight. However, for the sake of prospective parents and the outside world, the 'educational experiment at Dartington Hall' needed to be presented more formally.

The early prospectuses reflect among other influences Leonard's experience with Tagore, his enthusiasm for the Boy Scout movement's combination of practicality, co-operation and service, and Dorothy's contact with John Dewey. Michael Young, a pupil at the School in its early phase, has summed up the ideas laid out in the first prospectus in terms of four basic principles: "the curriculum should flow from the children's own interests; learning should, as much as possible, be by doing; adults should be friends rather than authority figures; and finally, the School should be self-governing." There was nothing particularly original about these guidelines, for they were very much in the general tradition of libertarian and child-centered education. Dartington was, however, offering something different and new: the School was not to be isolated from life, but *fully* integrated with the everyday world, and more so than any other school before it. There were to be no school buildings, and the Estate and countryside surrounding it would be the 'classrooms'. All the full-time workers on the Estate were regarded as members of the School's staff, and expected to contribute to the joint adventure in learning.

In accordance with the School's professed anti-authoritarianism and its status as a 'non-institution', there was, until 1928, no headmaster: the School was overseen by the Estate's Education Committee, which had a rotating Chairman, and was supposed to operate by majority vote. In practice, however, the Elmhirsts retained final control over everything — as was discovered on one particular occasion, when a committee decision to sack two Elmhirst appointees in the founders' absence was reversed on Leonard and Dorothy's return.

In addition to all the Estate workers, who were expected to pass on knowledge and skills, the Elmhirsts appointed a number of 'teachers': Wyatt Rawson, a former Cambridge friend of Leonard's; Marjorie Wise, a teacher who had trained at Teachers College in New York, where she had been strongly influenced by Dewey's ideas; Vic Elmhirst, Leonard's brother; and several others — more or less professional — who assisted with a number of activities including dance, painting, pottery and book-binding.

A stream of advisers came in from the United States, and offered early Dartington a remarkable range of expertise. These included Professor Lindeman from the New School of Social Work in New York; Professor Heuser from Cornell University, to design the new poultry unit; and Professor Roche from Cornell, to set up a workshop in which the children could learn various manual skills.

The School started with 10 pupils in September 1926 and numbers increased very gradually. At first the home atmosphere was very easily maintained. The style of the early days has been vividly described by Michael Young in his biography of the Elmhirsts. The children were very much left to their own devices, and they were able to choose which of the twelve departments on the Estate they wished to work with. 'Project work' on the Estate was supplemented by a small measure of academic tuition and regular talks and outings — many of which were organized by Leonard and Dorothy themselves, who as 'seniors', rather than the Lord and Lady of the Manor, were closely involved with the children during the early days.

The 'senior'/'junior' ratio was very favourable to the children, allowing for an unusual amount of individual attention. Much time was spent — naturally, given the emphasis on child-centeredness and the experimental nature of the process — on discussing, individually and collectively, what should be done. The local doctor, Dr. Williams, when asked to report on the School, even remarked that altogether too much time was devoted to self-government and child-centered decision-making, leaving the children visibly over-tired and unhealthy.

There were more fundamental difficulties, which began to emerge as the chaotic ferment and enthusiasm of early days gradually gave way to the demands of routine and the need for organisation. The adventure was not going smoothly, and the dreams laid out in the 1926 prospectus were not easily translated into the less dynamic language of reality. In the 1928, the Elmhirsts invited Professor A. T. Bonser and his wife, both of Teachers College in New York, to report on the School's progress.

The report was, as might be expected from two disciples of Dewey, generally sympathetic to the Elmhirsts' aims: the Bonsers did not condemn the notion of the Estate as an ideal bridge between learning and life, and they recognised the unique opportunities which Dartington offered to growing children. All depended, they wrote, on how that resource was used.

The Bonsers were professional educationists. As far as they were concerned, the Estate was to be used: it was to be seen as a school resource, rather than just a part of a whole to which 'juniors' and 'seniors' belonged. Their assumptions were, of course, quite understandable, and they had been invited to look at education rather than the whole Dartington experiment. Besides, the Elmhirsts themselves had inevitably found themselves drawing a line between learning and life — such established categories of thought were inescapable.

The Bonser Report stressed a number of major problems: the younger children (7–9 year-olds) did not fit at all well into ordinary Estate work, and they needed less complex and technical activities, although links could continue to be made with departmental heads. A teacher would be needed to take care of basic, child-orientated activities, such as simple spinning and weaving, modelling and pottery, the construction of toys, etc. Little connection was made between academic and Estate work for the older children, and the report stressed the need to make the two more relevant to each other through the appointment of a professionally trained 'co-ordinator', who would be in charge of making imaginative but necessary connections between specific activities on the Estate such as forestry or poultry-raising, and particular subject areas like geology, physics or history.

The central criticism — which emerged from the report, though veiled — had to do with the lack of professionalism which the Bonsers were bound to find in a project which so strongly rejected the traditional concepts of schooling. While some of the workers on the Estate were natural teachers, others must have found the 'juniors' difficult to accommodate; the 'juniors' were not apprentices in the traditionally recognised sense: they were not bound to a 'master' and were free to choose whatever they wished to do. The report remarked on the lack of punctuality amongst the 'juniors' and failure to keep appointments. The Bonsers also noted a tendency for projects to be abandoned before completion — an inevitable occurrence given the richness of the environment and the children's freedom.

According to the report, the educational experiment was too idealistic, assuming as it did that the 'juniors' could be integrated into Estate life without too much upheaval and in a way that would allow them to 'learn by doing'. The suggestions they made were designed to formalise the various loose relationships between 'juniors' and 'seniors', and while the Bonsers used those terms, it is clear from the report that they were more inclined to make the traditional distinctions between children who are learning and two kinds of adults: those who are trained to help children learn, and those who are skilled in other ways. Those distinctions were, of course, quite realistic, for, however much the Elmhirsts wished to avoid specialisation, they had chosen to work with an existing estate and with a 'staff' consisting in part of highly enthusiastic and committed amateurs, including themselves.

There were also the Estate workers, who must, on the whole, have found the experimental nature of the Elmhirsts' adventure difficult to understand — not least because they were used to children fitting in and being told what to do. The gap between the Elmhirsts' vision and the circumstances in which the experiment was being conducted was very large. Given the range of attitudes and priorities at Dartington in 1928, the Bonsers suggested a more formal integration of Estate and School. A degree of specialisation was unavoidable, but bridges between the distinct parts of the venture could be built and kept open. "A department head", they wrote, "should learn to expect to be called upon to teach from time to time, just as a teacher should expect to go to the field or shop now and then for a consultation with the students and

29

departmental heads. With this informal, yet systematic, type of teaching, there should soon disappear any self-consciousness on the part of either department heads or teachers in making every activity on the estate a possible opportunity for the boys and girls to learn to live more efficiently and more abundantly."

The Bonser Report marked the very beginning of a retreat from the amateur and de-institutionalised school towards a more conventional style — although the Bonsers' suggestions did emphasise the project's unique relationship to the Estate. By stressing the need for professionalism and formality — both of which were almost certainly necessary, given the particular circumstances at Dartington — the report was opening up the possibility for maximising the exploitation of the Estate's educational resources. However, it was unavoidably laying the ground at the same time for those divisions which would eventually develop, with the growth of School and Estate, into rigid compartments.

Shortly after the Bonsers handed in their report, the School began to change. Wyatt Rawson left Dartington, and Vic Elmhirst and John Wales became joint heads of the School — a concrete acknowledgement that such a school could no longer be seen as an integral and overlapping part of the Estate. The same year, the Education Committee was converted into an advisory body which met only occasionally. Although Michael Young writes of his delight at the freedom he experienced on his arrival in 1929, the School had already started moving towards more conventional teaching methods, and a more academic curriculum.

The Bonser Report was only one reflection of a more general trend at Dartington: the Estate was expanding fast, and the general policy of maximum integration which lay at the heart of the Tagore-inspired 'community' was beginning to be reappraised in the light of Estate politics and the Elmhirsts' increasing need and desire to delegate. A Management Committee was set up in 1927, and this eventually led to the establishment in 1929 of Dartington Hall Limited, a separate company which would control all the commercial enterprises. Dr. W. K. Slater was appointed as School Bursar and Estate Scientist, and the School accounts he produced came as a shock to all concerned. The time had come to consider the experiment quantitatively as well as qualitatively, and in neither respect did things look particularly bright.

The lines which have divided Dartington to this day — in terms of concepts, priorities and language — were beginning to be drawn. The intimacy of the early days, which derived from scale and from the Elmhirsts' charisma and infectious enthusiasm, was slowly and unavoidably disappearing. The conflict between commercial and educational priorities, and the inevitable tension between adventure and containment (a tension which became central to Dartington life), inevitably emerged — for the duality was inherent in the nature of the experiment and the realities of a working estate.

The Elmhirsts themselves were impressed by the conclusions of the Bonser Report, and they acknowledged the need for greater formality and professionalism. They soon decided to expand the School and to build accommodation for it outside the central courtyard area. They would appoint a headmaster and 'Director of Education' for the Estate. Both these decisions were to have fundamental and irreversible consequences. Once isolated in a separate building, the School would assume a special status and its own sense of 'place': in the first few years of the experiment that all-important sense of 'place' had been shared; now it was to be divided.

W. B. Curry's title 'Director of Education to the Social and Educational Experiment now being carried out at Dartington Hall', with its undertones of a 'learning community', does not really indicate just how deeply ideas about education on the Estate were changing. Curry, although responsible for other educational activities on the Estate, was to be headmaster of the School, and he played that role in a very independent manner, making the School very much his own.

Curry's School, which was to become one of the most highly regarded progressive co-educational boarding establishments in the world, owed as much to Bertrand Russell as it did to Dewey, and there was little evidence of Tagore's vision of a reintegrated community. The idea of 'learning by doing' continued to play an important part in School activities, but it was not as central as it

31

had been in the early years. A school farm and other facilities for learning practical tasks were set up. The idea of apprenticing pupils on the Estate itself was abandoned.

For Curry, the most important practical training the School could give was in the art of citizenship. He was a pacifist, believing in the need to settle differences by reason rather than force, and Dartington Hall School was to be a miniature of a perfect world, regulated by rational self-government and a free exchange between adults and children based on mutual respect, rather than hierarchical relationships.

It would be wrong to assume that the pull away from the centre was limited to the School and its individualistic and highly-talented new head. The creation of Dartington Hall Limited meant, in effect, that the Estate had become a series of commercial enterprises, although these continued to be called departments. "The Company", as Michael Young writes, "could not be lumbered with the education of funny-looking and funny-behaving children. How could the employees revere children as well as balance-sheets?" While in 1929 it had been possible to take a group photograph — including every member of the Estate as a group of 'seniors' and 'juniors' — Dartington had rapidly grown and begun to fragment, forming parts and groupings with separate identities. The feeling of place remained, however, as did personal allegiance to the founders — but there were now several 'Dartingtons' (and later yet more emerged), which made the fostering of a common purpose very difficult, if not impossible.

What then were the main obstacles to the reintegration of the Estate? It is impossible to explain the course of events in purely causal terms. Yet Dartington's early years cannot be solely dismissed, either, as an idealistic aberration; for they not only offer a means of understanding the relevance of Dartington's yearning towards integration, but also point very clearly to problems that are likely to affect *any* attempt at breaking down the barriers which our culture has erected between 'learning' and 'life'. While acknowledged as a failure, the early de-schooling experiment was remembered as a time in which integration had been nearly achieved; in the light of a certain nostalgia, the memory suggested a future practical possibility.

Quite apart from the various specifically educational problems outlined in the Bonser report, the entire Estate-wide experiment had suffered from severe overstretch: the Elmhirsts had not just embarked on an extraordinarily radical educational project, but they had moved into a range of dilapidated medieval buildings and taken on an estate that had suffered years of neglect. They were experimenting with new forms of dairy farming, poultry-rearing, forestry, rural industries, and small crafts. The scale and scope of the project was vast, which naturally limited the energy available for any given venture on the Estate.

There was also the fundamental contradiction hinted at above, between the cult of the child and the demands of running the Estate. Traditional apprenticeship has a great deal to do with discipline, as well as being based on an accepted hierarchical relationship between teacher and taught. It is assumed that there is value in continuity, and that particular skills and attitudes, essential to the community's survival and well-being, should be passed on. The exploratory kind of 'learning by doing', which places value on the child's innate potential and the need for a free and experimental approach, arises out of a philosophical outlook that challenges tradition and encourages change. At Dartington, the two currents met, and the resulting tension was unavoidable.

The clash of cultures which made a reintegration of the Estate so difficult, was also reflected (as it is today) in the different backgrounds of those who are involved in Dartington. There are those — mostly Devonian and country-bred — who have naturally gravitated towards the Estate because of proximity, family connections, or job availability; and there are those who have come, attracted by the Elmhirsts' idealism, and moved by a greater or lesser sense of the need to change the world. While the first group were by nature conservative and inclined towards a predictable and secure future, the latter were, on the whole, explorers, idealists and romantics, drawn by the promise of a return to some kind of Eden or the creation of a future Utopia. It was hardly surprising that the grafting of the Dartington experiment upon the Devon countryside should rapidly run into difficulties.

There was another serious contradiction, which appeared as soon as serious accounting began. This arose between the need for

Estate enterprises to be commercial, and the provision of a setting in which children could learn rather than be used as cheap or free labour. If the Elmhirsts' wished, among other things, to make life in the countryside viable, commercial success was not compatible with a child-centered notion of 'learning by doing', unless the departments in question were to be supported with adequate and long-term subsidy.

These inherent obstacles to integration were echoed by the manipulative aspect of the exercise, however much the Elmhirsts themselves mucked in and treated the early Estate as an extended family: the pre-industrial societies from which Tagore, Dewey, and no doubt Leonard and Dorothy Elmhirst too, drew their inspiration, had developed without articulated intent, in gradual and appropriate response to small communities' survival and spiritual needs. This wish to revitalise was, however, interventionist and idealistic; the Elmhirsts translated it into an actual experiment through the creative use of inherited money as well as an extraordinary combination of imagination and courage. There was never, however, the kind of commitment which goes with a struggle for survival, where 'learning by doing' becomes a necessity rather than an ideal, and integration is a natural product of collaborative striving in the face of adversity. In that they were able to experiment, the Elmhirsts betrayed a measure of detachment from the Estate. Such a detachment was an inevitable by-product of a vision which enabled them to see beyond the restrictions of the everyday and means which allowed them to act as if such limitations did not exist.

The vision which inspired the Elmhirsts came from beyond the realm of the concrete and possible, as do all such creative intuitions. Leonard and Dorothy were driven by a need, shared by many others of their time, to create meaningful structures around them, and to seek alternatives to the fragmentation of urban existence. The pattern that guided them called for the reintegration of learning, life, and place, but they were probably only dimly aware of the full implications (and contradictions) of the dream that inspired them. Besides, they were not just dreamers, and the practicalities of the project, once it was established, provided a new focus for their energy and enthusiasm.

The realisation of the original ideas behind the 'Dartington experiment' would have involved no less than a radical change in world-view, a re-focusing and re-structuring of perspectives, values and priorities. The Elmhirsts, and those who have been drawn to Dartington over the years, have all sensed something, however small, of the need for different attitudes to the world around us. But the Estate's potential, as ground for such a reorientation has never achieved more than a haunting intimation of possibilities always projected into the future, forever drawing people to Dartington and stimulating experiment and change.

It is only possible to hint at the nature of such a cultural and metaphysical realignment: to lay it down or codify it involves using the very language and concepts that such an alternative seeks to transcend. It is over-definition, the burden of dogma and the linear goal-orientation of reforming crusades from which this different perspective turns away — for it is rooted in stability, tradition and place rather than movement, change and progress; it values multiplicity, connection and interdependence as much as division, individuality and duality. The process of reorientation requires a reappraisal of the dominant scientific and materialistic world-view. Yet we are so conditioned by this perspective, that change is slow and halting.

The 'educational experiment' of Dartington's early years drew its inspiration and strength from the image of a reintegrated community. Within three years, the inspiration had become entwined in the web of circumstance, transformed by the heavy weight of orthodoxy and thwarted by its own contradictions. There remained, however, a powerful after-image, which has been repeatedly projected over the years upon the Dartington Estate and lingers to this day. The idea of Dartington's hidden potential, and the promise of integration have survived as strong guiding themes: the Estate as classroom, and the impulse to take 'learning' out into the world, to see education as 'of life' rather than 'about life'. It is in the light of this that all Dartington's later experiments with 'learning by doing' should be understood.

DOROTHY ELMHIRST, quoted in Michael Young's biography The Elmhirsts of Dartington, *describes evening activities typical of the School's first few years:*

Our evenings have become delightfully social. On Mondays we all get together to sew, staff and children, often to the accompaniment of song or the gramophone. On Tuesdays we have a Dancing Class, composed of Seniors, the older Juniors, the gardener's children, the maids of our household, and our second man. It is a most wonderful and unique affair, about thirty of us in all. We are learning the charleston, the tango, and all the latest tricks of the trade, and even Whitney has decided that we are thoroughly up to date. On Wednesday we used to have chorus singing, but recently science has encroached on art, and Mr. Heuser (our poultry expert from Cornell) has been dissecting chickens and giving the most thrilling demonstrations in physiology and biology ... For the discussions we all gather around the fire on the floor and thrash out some subject like the meaning of drudgery, or the consequences of punishment, or what religion means to us individually ... Last week Leonard read aloud a sketch of the life of Buddha.

Michael Young, a Dartington Hall Trustee since the 1940s, came to the School after the Elmhirsts had begun to steer it back towards a more conventionally 'institutional' line. Until W. B. Curry took over, however, learning by doing remained a central idea. Michael Young writes:

I became an apprentice in the orchards and, when I was not fiddling with carburettors, 'life' was picking up and bagging apples for cider-making. I had an exercise book in which I drew pictures of trees, with all the branches cut through with lines to show where they should be pruned, looking like a manual of acupuncture. That lasted six months, until Tasmania faded as an ambition and my grandfather refused to pay any more. But I was able to stay on. I got a scholarship, or perhaps I should say a motorbikeship ... Fruit was followed by poultry. A group of boys and girls set up a tiny poultry co-operative called Darfowls, with me as Secretary. We entered into a formal lease (learning law too from the poultry project?) with Mr. Elmhirst for the ground on which the hen-house stood. It was strange to see Leonard called that in the

36

lease. The eggs were candled and sold to the school kitchen at whatever the market price was that week in Totnes. At the end of a year's work, supervised by a real poultryman, each member of the co-operative got a dividend of four shillings. Apart from some bookkeeping I learnt I could no more hope to be a good farmer of poultry than I could of fruit: I could candle splendidly; but I could not bear to wring the chickens' necks, although I tried and tried to bring myself and the hen to the crunch. From poultry I progressed to the architect's office to learn draughtsmanship, designing one paper house after another; and always there was what was later called 'Useful Work', felling and thinning trees in the wood for whose care the school was responsible on Gallow's Hill. The little world had a great deal of variety given to it by practitioners who were not so much teachers as doers. I learnt a vital negative lesson, about things I was not capable of doing. I could not wring a neck, I could not dance, I could not design a house, I could not grow fruit, I could not make money from hens, I could not stand next to a naked girl of my own age in a shower without being startled; the beginning, I realised, of a much longer list.

(Michael Young, *The Elmhirsts of Dartington*, 1982.)

The Yorkshire Project. Some of the ROSLA youngsters on a mine visit.

CHAPTER THREE

De-schooling in the 1960s

THE YORKSHIRE AND SICILY PROJECTS

T HE ESSENTIAL CHARACTERISTIC of the school that evolved at
Dartington under W. B. Curry, and later under his succes-
sors, Hu and Lois Child, lay in a wholehearted commitment to
the individual. This child-centered ethic ran counter to the
conformism of a highly competitive mass society. The School
provided a privileged and sheltered environment for the development of each pupil.

All schools, whether conventional or progressive, involve a
degree of separation from the world at large but Dartington, as
a fee-paying boarding school in a rural area and with its
emphasis on individual freedom, was more isolated than most.
Although in the early days the Elmhirsts aspired to minimise
the boundaries between School and Estate, for most of its life
the School tended to turn inwards, cultivating its own unique
atmosphere and relationships.

The curriculum covered much the same ground as in
ordinary schools, with definite subject areas, and firm divisions between arts and sciences, the academic and the practical. There was more project-work than in more conventional
schools: there was a school farm, which in its most flourish-
ing days kept the establishment in vegetables; and non-
academic pursuits such as pottery, art and music were considered as valuable to the development of the child as more
conventional educational subjects. The School had become,
however, a separate institution with little except history to

connect it to Tagore and Dewey and to the Elmhirsts' original vision.

With Royston Lambert's appointment as headmaster in 1968, the School entered a new phase. The cultural stirrings of the 1960s encouraged a radical reappraisal of institutional forms and of authority. It was around this time that Ivan Illich and Everett Reimer published widely influential attacks on institutionalised education and the school as a forcing-house which isolated pupils from the world and attempted to fill them with information that was as packaged as it was inappropriate. 'De-schooling' became a familiar slogan reflecting, collectively, a deep unease with one of the most cherished goals of social progress. The idea of de-schooling emerged with an increasing awareness of the gigantic gap that yawned between the rituals of school and the demands of the world.

The 'greening' of the 1960s harked back, in many ways, to Romanticism, the Arts and Crafts movement, and the Fellowship of the New Life. The time was ripe for a rediscovery of Dartington's own debt to that tradition, and while the projects undertaken during Royston Lambert's headship appeared, superficially, to be very different from those of Dartington's early days as they stressed the breaking of class as much as institutional barriers, they nevertheless reflected a similar concern for social and cultural reintegration, the crucial role of 'learning by doing', and the need to blur or remove the barriers between school and the world.

"I have just become headmaster of a school. If things go well, by the time I leave, there might not be much of a conventional school left for me to headmaster: I hope to have become non-head of the first anti-school in the country, the first of many." So wrote Royston Lambert, with characteristic panache, in *New Society*, shortly after his appointment at Dartington. He went on to describe his plans for the de-construction of the School, opening it up in every direction, with a particular emphasis on the initiation of school-leavers to the adult world.

In this article and in the W. B. Curry Memorial Lecture which he gave at Exeter University in 1972, Royston made very clear his educational outlook and plans. While being in sympathy with the libertarian basis of Dartington's school, he was acutely conscious of the institution's alienation from the world around it. All schools, as far as Royston Lambert was concerned, whether progressive or orthodox, presented certain inescapable features: schools institutionalised and segregated a particular age-group; the institution, by its very nature, determined that legitimate activities be largely educational, imposed certain social groupings, and set limits around the use of time, as well as fragmenting the learning process itself into artificially separate subjects.

But Dartington, in particular, with its beautiful rural setting and catering to the children of a privileged class, presented in extreme form the characteristics of an isolated 'hot house society', as Royston Lambert had characterised the boarding schools in the title of his recently published book. Dartington "may be more socially exclusive", Lambert wrote, "than many public schools, because it draws not from the whole upper class, but from one of its sub-cultures (the creative, permissive intelligentsia)". Royston was concerned, above all, with the School's social isolation, not so much in terms of the Estate, but in relation to the majority who could not afford fee-paying boarding education. He believed that it was crucial, too, for progressive methods — which had so far only influenced the state systems at the primary level — to be tried out with adolescents of all social backgrounds. Was the progressive ethic, Lambert asked, in conflict with ordinary life, or could it be used to help prepare *all* young people for the world?

Dartington's new headmaster focused on three aspects of reintegration: the need to open the School out into the world, allowing for a two-way exchange; the need to break down the accepted divisions between school and work or life; and the need to broaden the School's base across existing class boundaries, and to explore ways of relating to the state system. It was Dartington's financial independence which made experimentation possible, and freedom and privilege could only be justified, he felt, if it could be shown to genuinely serve the needs of a wider community.

In practice, Royston set up a number of adventurous projects designed to break open the school boundaries or in his own words "to turn the school inside-out". Of these, the Yorkshire and Sicily projects were probably the most remarkable, although they were only parts of a wider scheme which was intended to transform the School from a predominantly inward-looking institution into an open-ended nexus of projects involving an unusually broad range of participants.

THE YORKSHIRE PROJECT

"THE SCHOOL should come to terms with urban living", Royston Lambert wrote in *New Society* in January 1969, shortly after his appointment, "it should sprout a branch in a city centre. Indeed it should offer its students the widest possible choice and experience, it should look abroad, and construct opportunities for them to study, live, and work in other cultures." The 'city centre' idea was never translated into a concrete venture, but the Yorkshire project gave the School strong links with a very different place and culture — a sharp contrast to Dartington's idyllic Devon setting.

The project was centered on the mining community of Conisbrough, six miles south of Doncaster, at the eastern end of the South Yorkshire coal-field. The area was suffering from considerable unemployment, and the many other side-effects of an industry that was being rapidly run down. The terraces of houses owned by the National Coal Board near the Denaby Main colliery were recognised as some of the worst slums in Yorkshire.

In 1969 Royston Lambert established an exchange scheme between Dartington and Northcliffe School, a Secondary Modern school in Conisbrough. The scheme was assisted by the West Riding Education Authority and enabled Northcliffe children to attend Dartington Hall School for anything from a week to two years. In return, students from Dartington went to Yorkshire, though usually for shorter periods. In both cases the adjustment process was by no means easy — but then neither was it supposed to be. The project in Yorkshire would never have happened without the imaginative support of Alec Clegg, then Chief Education Officer for the West Riding, and later a Dartington Hall Trustee.

As many other Dartington experiments, the scheme was never properly monitored. This is surprising, considering Dartington's self-image as a laboratory for new ideas. It is therefore difficult to draw any precise conclusions as to its longer-term value. It is clear, however, that it must, at the very least, have broadened the horizons of those taking part.

In order to provide a base for Dartington's 'study-visits' to Yorkshire, the Dartington Hall Trust bought 'the Terrace', in Conisbrough. In 1972, Pat and Dick Kitto, both of whom had been involved with the School at Dartington, moved in as wardens. They took over the running of the sixth form visits to the Yorkshire outpost. The Terrace could accommodate up to 16 children in three dormitories, and five to six adults. There were also a small number of seminar or activity rooms and two acres of land. These courses were very much prototypes for the 'urban studies' approach to project-based learning which became more widely used during the 1970s. The programme included visits to coal pits, a steel works and woollen mill. The Dartington students interviewed people living in Sheffield's high-density flats, and took part in 'seminars' in the streets of Conisbrough with the help of local teachers and residents. In the evenings Conisbrough housewives, councillors and pensioners came to the Terrace to meet the Dartington group. The Terrace offered, at this time, a remarkable move from the previous isolation of Dartington, and a brief but revealing glimpse of a radically different environment and culture.

In 1973, with the raising of the school-leaving age (ROSLA) to 16, the Terrace's use was to be greatly extended, (up to that point it had only been occupied from time to time). For Royston Lambert, the extra year at school represented a misguided further retreat from the transition from school to work: "in the name of equality of opportunity," he wrote, "another whole age stratum is being drawn into the institution ..." Dartington's outpost in the Yorkshire mining town would provide an ideal setting for an "alternative to school", for those Northcliffe children "who have hitherto been indifferent or antagonistic to their schooling", but were expected to stay on because of the raising of the school-leaving age. Although the ROSLA Scheme in Yorkshire was at the outset only on offer to those who would previously have left school at 15, it was conceived as a pilot scheme that might be replicable in other parts of the country, and with other age-groups.

The Scheme was designed as a kind of initiation into the world beyond school, an initiation that would stimulate the emergence of each youngster's sense of self and others, and his/her ability to make choices. The Terrace would not be run as a school, and the ROSLA youngsters would be expected to take an active part in decisions that affected them.

Life at the Terrace was not to be fragmented according to an externally imposed time-table or subject areas, but was to flow naturally, from task to task, encompassing a wide range of activities, many of which might not, in the conventional sense, be defined as educational. The youngsters were to look after domestic chores, and everyone would be involved in earning money in some way, as well as taking part in some kind of social or community work. Royston Lambert placed great emphasis, too, on the arts and crafts, hoping that a year at the Terrace would offer plenty of opportunities for practical exploration, as well as broadening the youngsters' cultural experience in every possible way.

Royston hoped that, just as Dartington Hall School was to open itself up to the world, the Terrace would remain as free of boundaries as possible, with the youngsters aware of the wealth of resources beyond its walls. He wanted the building to be a living community that welcomed not just those on the ROSLA Scheme, but young wage-earners and other adults from the community as well. Royston Lambert also hoped that much could be made of the connection with Dartington, and that pupils from the Dartington School would become involved in activities at the Terrace.

The first group of ROSLA youngsters joined the Scheme in 1973. All 15 of them were boys from Northcliffe School who would have stayed at the school until Easter or Summer 1974, but were not thought likely to gain '0' levels or worthwhile CSE results, or to benefit from conventional schooling.

Royston Lambert had originally intended to run the ROSLA

Scheme himself but, as it turned out, he was unable to do so. Neal Fitzgerald was seconded from Northcliffe School to take charge of the Scheme, and he was assisted by Ken Hosie of the Terrace staff. The Terrace's wardens, Pat and Dick Kitto naturally played a crucial part in the project, while still organising the course visits from Dartington. Arthur Young, Northcliffe's highly sympathetic headmaster, was in overall control of the Scheme. The ROSLA Scheme was partly financed by the Dartington Hall Trust, who owned the building and paid most of the Terrace staff's salaries, as well as making a grant towards the conversion of the Terrace coach-house. The West Riding Education Authority paid for one member of staff. Some day-to-day running costs were covered by money earned by the group on outside jobs. The future of the Scheme depended, clearly, on continuing sympathy and support from the Trust and the Education Authority.

From the first term, the fifteen youngsters became involved in a number of practical projects: the coach house was converted for use as a workshop and rest room for the group. Some of the youngsters looked after two allotments, which included a greenhouse, chicken shed and rabbit hutches. Others were occupied with decoration and maintenance work in the main Terrace building.

Regular expeditions were organised, always in response to the group's own inclinations, rather than a pre-established educational programme. These included visits to art exhibitions, Grimsby Docks and an army training centre. A number of the youngsters took part in outside courses: metalwork at Dartington for some, rock climbing and car maintenance locally for others. A walking and camping trip along the Pennine Way with a group of Dartington students was also set up. A group of boys made regular weekly visits — on their own initiative — to a local hospital for the 'sub-normal', and others were involved in the production of a Mummers play that was performed in a number of local schools and subsequently taken on a tour of North Devon.

Links with Northcliffe School were strong, and some of the youngsters chose to attend specific classes, and half of the

Terrace group in the first year took part in games at the school. The close connection with Northcliffe provided a strong and natural link with a key institution in the local community, as well as broadening Northcliffe's own sense of a school's identity.

It had been Royston Lambert's original intention that participants in the ROSLA Scheme should find full- or part-time work, or at the very least 'work experience'. One boy was taken on at a local garage, but had to leave because of insurance problems raised by the new government Works Experience Bill. Later, the youngsters set up their own furniture restoration business, and some of them worked for a local antique dealer.

While local people at first, understandably felt suspicious of the goings-on at the Terrace, relations rapidly improved. "It is evident", an early report on the Scheme pointed out, "that the practicality of the scheme appeals to a great many people, as they see it as a way of preparation for the youngsters' working life. Many local tradesmen have given practical advice, help, and gifts of material." It was quite natural for people to rally round: these were local people trying to make good, and the common adversity facing all those who lived in a rapidly declining industrial area provided very strong ground for active mutual support.

In the light of this kind of community spirit, Dartington's own continuing difficulties with creating an integrated environment in and around the estate in Devon were thrown into relief — for there has rarely been a comparable harmony between locally-perceived needs, the aims of the Elmhirsts or the Trust, and the specific projects launched at Dartington or in the immediate neighbourhood. The more recent Work Experience and Postern programmes have to some extent tapped such a sense of common need. Yet at Conisbrough, Tagore's ideals, stripped of romanticism, were finding expression in direct answer to basic needs: needs which could be met relatively simply and with tangible results.

The Scheme's role as a context for 'initiation' into self-awareness and responsibility was central: the youngsters recognised this inwardly, with emerging confidence, as did their parents, teachers and the Career Officers who met them. In providing a setting which enabled the youngsters to start taking responsibility for their own lives, the ROSLA project was filling a vacuum that families, schools and the work-place were for a variety of reasons unable to cope with. Instinctively, the community around the Terrace recognised this, welcoming and supporting the project for its role in helping transform children into adults with a growing sense of themselves.

The youngsters that joined the Scheme were selected from those who found school most difficult. They had mostly been anonymous members of large classes, lacking in self-confidence, and with very low expectations of themselves. Some had been in trouble with the law, and several came with a background of truancy. They had had very little real contact with adults, and most of this was experienced as rather negative. On first arriving at the Terrace, the shock was considerable. As Ken Hosie of the Terrace staff noted at the time, the youngsters found themselves in a bewildering situation: they were more free than they had ever been at home or school, and adults showed respect for them and listened. They were, in another sense, less free, because they were unable to retreat into anonymity, as they were being cared for every minute of the day by a comparatively high ratio of adults.

After a period of disorientation and chaos, the group gradually developed a sense of coherence and purpose; the youngsters began to express themselves in constructive ways. Group discussions which had been very sticky at first became increasingly lively. As attitudes changed, the quality of the youngsters' work and their commitment to it returned as well. At the end of the first term, the local employment officer recorded that the young people interviewed well, and on the whole better than their peer group. They knew what they wanted and expressed their feelings clearly. They took the interview seriously and he was struck by the fact that whatever the youngsters wanted to do, they were in each case capable of doing. There was very little fantasy about what kind of jobs they wanted. He stated that each participant in the scheme "had an individuality of his own which was often backed up by a very real sense of humour." "Boys like this", he added, "should have little difficulty getting jobs as they interviewed so well, and had obviously benefitted from the practical skills they had learned during the term."

By September of 1974, the future of the ROSLA Scheme at the Terrace was uncertain. Neal Fitzgerald and Ken Hosie had left, though the former was soon replaced by Jerry McLister. The Kittos stayed until April 1975, when they were replaced by Stuart Lindeman, a Northcliffe teacher, who later transferred to Aller Park, the Junior and Middle School at Dartington, and was a central figure in the Postern Programme.

The Dartington Hall Trust decided to withdraw its backing of the Scheme at the end of 1974. The economic crisis of 1973/4 had severely hit Dartington, and Royston Lambert's almost unchecked expansionist regime at the School had created budget deficits which the Trust could not support for long. There was retrenchment all round. The re-organisation of local government in 1974 had also removed Northcliffe and the Terrace from the sympathetic control of West Riding Education Authority. Doncaster, the new authority, was Conservative-controlled and naturally less inclined to back small experiments which might be seen to undermine traditional ideas about authority and conventional schooling.

Although Dartington pulled out of the ROSLA Scheme, the exchange scheme with Northcliffe School continued well into the 1980s, though on a progressively decreasing scale. These exchanges, though providing a valuable opportunity for students from very different backgrounds to broaden their horizons, represent only the faintest shadow of the collaborative de-institutionalisation originally envisaged by Royston Lambert.

After 1974, Royston Lambert's plans for an anti-school and an institutional explosion into the world beyond Dartington were abandoned. The School, once again, drew inwards. The aims of the Terrace, however, and particularly the style and objectives of the ROSLA Scheme were soon to be explored again by the Trust, with plans for a 'vocational training centre', the Work Experience Project and the Postern Programme.

'Learning by doing' in the context of the ROSLA Scheme was not so much about acquiring specific skills, but trying to 'animate' young people with a poor sense of self-esteem, who had hitherto been programmed for submission to authority and conformity. Orthodox education — with its transmission of knowledge within an artificial, specialised, and socially isolated setting — produced 'successes', who had willingly taken on the educational package, and 'failures', who had, in one way or another, refused schooling. The ROSLA Scheme provided something radically different, for it was concerned instead with initiation into self-awareness: the prerequisite for free and responsible participation in society. It is impossible to teach initiation into adulthood in the classroom. It can only emerge through experience and in a context that is not sheltered from the conflicts and pressures of the world — a kind of half-way house in which new roles, attitudes and modes of self-expression can be explored.

Beyond the Classroom

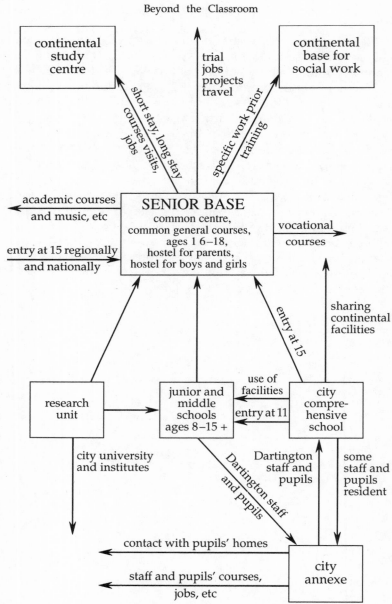

Illustration for 'What Dartington will do' by Royston Lambert in New Society, *30th Jan '69*

'A SCHOOL WITH A BASE IN SOCIETY'

ROYSTON LAMBERT took over the headmastership of the School in 1969. He came to Dartington from a research post at Cambridge; it was partly this degree of distance from institutional education which allowed him to suggest radical changes at the School. In the 1972 W. B. Curry Memorial Lecture, he laid down some guidelines for what was to become the Yorkshire Project.

This experiment is based on no general political doctrines and is not intended to shake society to its foundations as are contemporary American theories of de-schooling. Indeed it does not derive from dogma at the macrocosmic level but from pragmatic observation of the actual needs of children over some years, and in particular of the working-class adolescents who will form this kind of group. There will be about thirty of them, the size of an ordinary class, and they will come from those who have hitherto been indifferent or antagonistic to their schooling. The following nine principles and approaches will be tried in an effort to fulfil the aim of all education of developing the personality of the child, his skills and values, so as to enable him to make the best of his own qualities and of the changing world in which he lives.

1. Young people need the continuous and sympathetic support and guidance of an adult (or adults) other than their parents. This most schools simply cannot and do not provide as teachers are mainly concerned to transmit information or elicit skills. One adult will be the focal point of this group and it will be his job to see each person privately every week about their progress, prospects and problems and get to know their parents and family situation thoroughly. Otherwise the job of the adult is to facilitate whatever the group or its individuals are doing, to activate parents, outside adults, facilities (not necessarily schools) or resources and to guide and sustain the group as a whole, drawing out the implications and interconnections of whatever is being done.

2. Children need a base other than home from which to operate but this base need not be a special institution designed, equipped and removed, as are most schools. In this case the base will be a house near the centre of a town with space for private reading, some indoor recreation, beds, and some outdoor and workshop

space. Grandiose premises are not needed and much smaller places than the one we are going to use would be quite appropriate.

3. Most young people develop beneficially by interaction within a group or groups of other young people but need not be exclusively confined to this age texture. Much of the work and activity of this group would involve working alongside adults from all walks of life or working with other age groups such as the very young and the very old.

4. For their fullest development young people should have a real and not sham share in decisions which affect them, should be able to interact openly and fearlessly with adults who guide them on terms of equality, should be free in matters of personal self expression and taste and be subject to democratic procedures where their freedom impinges on that of others. In other words the progressive ethic will be thoroughly applied and all issues, plans and progress will be regularly discussed and decisions, including financial ones, be taken by the group. This itself will be the main educational experience for everyone as skills of rationalisation and communication are so sadly lacking among the children concerned.

5. The division of time into fragmented, sequential programmes and the distinction between school and ordinary life are arbitrary, dictated by the needs of organisations not of the people within them. There will be in this group no compulsory hours of attendance, not 9 a.m. to 4 p.m., no set holidays and no set terms and individuals or groups may be active at any time of the day, evening or weekend. In general, activity will be continuously followed through until a natural pause is reached or the task is completed, it will not be divided into half an hour periods of this and half an hour periods of that or an afternoon of the other.

6. The growth of personality, values and skills can best be promoted for children like this by working through the context and content of situations which they perceive as real life ones and relevant, using the content to increase their awareness, discrimination and implications, rather than using separate institutional processes with their artificial life and rituals, regulated procedures, traditional subject matter and systematised programmes of learning and instruction.

Subject to the further ideas and the agreement of the group, activity with them would be based round the following:

(a) The group would have a float of money, quite a considerable sum, for which it would be responsible.

(b) It would look after the house and buy, organise and prepare communal meals when it was agreed that they would be held.

(c) Economic activity, such as part-time jobs would be permitted and watched and evaluated by the group. Many children have part-time jobs at present which schools ignore. Everyone would participate in some economic activity to raise money for individuals and for the group's own activities. Such activities might include (according to the youngsters with whom I have already discussed it) window cleaning syndicates, a baby-sitting service, running an allotment and a hen-house and selling the produce at a local market weekly, car washing, produce and craft making and selling, folk singing groups, decorating and the like. The group would decide what ventures to back, how much to invest, what wages to pay its members and what to do with the excess proceeds. This small-scale economic activity builds on what many children, especially truanters in this area, already do and would develop all the skills involved in larger economic processes and contact with a wide range of adults.

(d) Unpaid work of a social service kind would be done but more thoroughly and over longer stretches of time than school curricula usually permit. There would be work with the young (including a playgroup at the house), with the old, with people in institutions, reclamation of the local environment and work with animals, including animal banks, an animal shelter, help with the PDSA and so on. Again the group will decide what ventures to back and how to invest its members' time and money and to evaluate the progress of each project.

(e) Cultural activity would fall into three basic kinds: (i) creative work by individuals or the group including the arts, dressmaking, wood and metalwork and also group drama, puppetry, folk singing, poetry sessions, some of which would be developed for social service projects, (ii) the whole group would explore the culture of its area and then evaluate it, the commercial culture of youth, the more indigenous culture such as working men's clubs, trades unions, the numerous voluntary and religious bodies and attention would be paid to informal cultural groups and rituals, (iii) using the immensely rich resources of the nearby cities, universities, galleries, country houses and events, the group would have to encounter cultural styles other than that so uniform and so inward-looking as that of the particular community. Full use will be made of the Dartington connection in this respect by visits there and by involving Dartington pupils in the experiment itself.

(f) From all of this, certain basic themes will come up which will be regularly pursued by research by individuals and by sub-groups, guided by the adult, reporting to the main group for discussion and using facilities such as local libraries, individuals, voluntary organisations and parents as well as the school centre itself. The following are likely to arise: (i) issues of personal relations and sex, (ii) ethical problems, (iii) spiritual and religious problems, (iv) economic problems, especially the unemployment which threatens everyone of them and their fathers, (v) social problems such as violence, (vi) political issues and current affairs, (vii) issues of science and technology and their effects.

7. A wide range of facilities would be used. Of these the school itself might be one conceived as a resource centre and indeed some students might well subscribe to an actual course at the school using facilities otherwise not available, as for example a course in languages or metalwork. But other resources would also be used such as public libraries, factories, commercial enterprises and a wide variety of voluntary organisations, so little used at the moment by schools, and staffed by adults who are eager and able to offer help and practical first hand experience. Among these there will also be the many working men's clubs in the area in question, a source of funds, adult help and experience not hitherto tapped by the conventional educational set-up but at the heart of the local culture.

8. No distinction would be made between those leaving and those not yet legally able to take a full-time job. If, when the law allows, members leave for full-time work, they can still remain part of and involved with the group as long as they wish, bringing back to it their own brand of experience. One of the most absurd and cruel aspects of school is the way on leaving the young person walks out of the formal educational process as though at sixteen society has nothing more formally to offer its young. Ultimately the group might contain quite a proportion of younger wage earners.

9. For physical activities the group might plan its own expeditions, join school teams and use local non-school clubs and facilities.

There would, using the Dartington connection, be expeditions down there for purposes concerned with the work and any other ones the group cares to organise and finance. There would also be residential experience available at the house.

LIFE AT THE TERRACE

*P*AT AND DICK KITTO, *who had been on the staff of Dartington Hall School went up to Conisbrough (Yorkshire) in 1974 to take over the Terrace, one of the School's 'social work bases'. Pat wrote about the Terrace in an article published in the Times Educational Supplement in November 1974. Two extracts from the piece follow.*

"I don't see why we should have to pay for Kev's bust cable. If he'd left his bike in a car park and it had happened, no one would have paid for it."

"Aye, but it weren't in a car park. Kev belongs to this group and someone from here did it."

"We don't know who, though."

"That's no reason why Kev should have to pay for it himself."

"I'm not going to pay for it, anyroad", says Robby in his usual forthright way.

"Nor me", says Fred, jumping on Robby's wagon.

"Tha's only t'monk on..."

"But what'll we do if Robby don't give nothing?"

This conversation took place a year ago at a meeting of the ROSLA Alternative to School Scheme in Conisbrough near Doncaster. The boys shouted across the room to each other. There was a feeling of excitement, of getting to grips with real matters of principle. The excitement was unusual. At the first two meetings of the Alternative to School year, the boys had few contributions to make. Egged on to speak, their replies were: "Not bothered" or "If you say so". Or even: "You're t'gaffers, you tell us what to do."

But this time things were different. Neal, one of the teachers, was given a pound for the three or four boys who had done a little job for a miner who helps us on the allotment. Neal divided the money between the boys and they spent it on cigarettes and sweets. The other boys thought that unfair. Any money given to a member of the group belonged to them all.

Some of the boys defended the action, the others pointed out the injustice of it. Neal said he would pay the pound into the fund himself. "He can't do that," said Peter. "It wouldn't be fair. He's made a mistake: but we all make mistakes at times." (An amazing remark from the boy who is always first to point out other people's mistakes). "I vote we let him off and forget it." So Neal was let off by a general vote.

Then followed the discussion about the broken cable, the result of which was that everyone agreed to pay 2p out of their own pocket. Everyone except Robby. In the end, someone let Robby's tyres down.

That particular kind of rough justice died down as the meetings became more alive and useful and the boys were able to use them to express their feelings about the group and the staff. For instance, there was an occasion later in the year when some of the boys did not turn out to help with the potato picking at a local farm. All the money they earned went into the group funds, either to finance the group or for outside activities.

If some of the group were dragging their feet, the others could be seen to be working for the idle ones, a point quickly realised by everyone. Some strong feelings were expressed about this particular matter, though little punishment was exacted from them. During the year this generosity actually increased. It was not unusual to hear the meeting express the view that although Tom had not pulled his weight on the last job, on the job before that he had done more than his fair share.

A change of attitude became obvious throughout the year. From talking in grunts and monosyllables, punctuated by punches and grabs at the nearest person, they began to talk freely, make comments, and even undertake abstract arguments, especially if they concerned money or power.

LET ME QUOTE one of the many experiences from which we learnt. After a fairly heavy working week, the boys decided during a meeting that they were fed up with work and for the week following would do nothing. The adults, outvoted anyway, agreed. It seemed at the time that the more reliable boys would in fact go on working. They did not. The pressures from the others were too heavy. No one worked.

The week stretched from one endless day to the next. A record player rasped, cards were played, cigarettes smoked, the boys sighed with boredom. Animals were left unfed and relationships with the staff deteriorated. The boys felt guilty, the staff were fretful. The workshop became incredibly dirty and untidy. It looked as though any discipline which had been gained for the group had gone forever. Not one of the boys truanted; that might have been too easy.

Meanwhile, a residential course was in progress. The students in the house were trying to work; the ROSLA group were doing nothing. At the Friday meeting at which the week was to be discussed, some headmasters visited the place in all its messy glory. They were anxious to know what the staff thought might be the outcome of the meeting. The staff could not say; they did not know. All they decided was to keep quiet and make no comment and let the boys have their say.

But from the first words of the meeting, it was clear what the outcome was to be. The boys declared they were fed up. They had smoked too many cigarettes, played too many card games, and they did not really like doing nothing all week. They preferred to work with the staff, they said. They felt bad about the relationships which had developed; they felt even worse about the animals. Everything was to be as before, except that they wanted a half day off each week to do their own thing — either reading, walking or working at something for themselves. And it has been that way ever since.

HOW IS ONE TO JUDGE education in terms such as these? The people involved in the group are convinced of its educational value with its emphasis on the boys learning about themselves and their capacities within the group. In contrast to school, where middle-class values prevail, an attempt was made to reaffirm the boys' own background and values, especially by involving local parents and groups. At the same time, attempts were made to widen their experience and attitudes by, for example, meeting pupils from Dartington, visiting art galleries, and making excursions to the Scottish Highlands.

Some of these experiences the boys found difficult to accept, and in some cases — on the excursions to the Highlands and to London — they displayed entrenched attitudes and values. Perhaps the adults were too keen to impose their own ideas and standards on the group, making the children of this northern mining town feel their own values were being criticised and threatened.

In such a scheme, where a new approach of learning is the basis, the values of those concerned in the work are inevitably criticised and a great deal of self-examination is necessary. It is a delicate balance in education between affirming a person's life style and leading him to new experiences. Because of the diverse nature of work, at least two staff were needed for 15 children. This gives grounds for more criticism. But if this is seen as an experiment from which we can learn something about education, a generous staff ratio is essential until the lessons have been learnt.

THE SICILY PROJECT

T HE IDEA of taking the school beyond the geographical and cultural boundaries of the estate was central to Royston's plan for reinterpreting the role of 'school'. But other accepted boundary-lines needed to be broken: one of these was the notion that, once a sixth form student had finished with 'A' levels or university entrance, she or he should make a clean break with school. "The Terrace", Lambert suggested in his W. B. Curry Memorial Lecture, "should welcome regular visits from our former members of the ROSLA Scheme, as well as young wage-earners who had recently left Northcliffe School."

The Sicily Project, while different in many respects, shared this half-way house ambition: it was planned as a 'social work base abroad', but it would also provide graduates from Foxhole (Dartington's senior school) with a stepping-stone into adult life, an alternative to the traditional year's 'bumming around' or voluntary service. The project also appealed to Lambert's strong social and political convictions: Dartington Hall School needed to break the isolation of its privileged rural and class status; Sicily, like Yorkshire, could help to open the school up.

The idea of a 'social work base abroad' harked back, however remotely, to Dartington's beginnings: Leonard Elmhirst's work with Rabindranath Tagore in Bengal paved the way for the Elmhirsts' plan to revitalise the Estate. Direct experience of a more integrated traditional culture had provided Leonard with a kind of template for the fuller life that he hoped would flow from a re-energised Dartington.

Leonard Elmhirst had maintained strong links with India and had, over the years, acted as a consultant to a number of development projects in the sub-continent. In the 1960s Dartington renewed its contact with the Third World by establishing an Africa Trust which backed cultural projects in Tanzania. At the end of the decade, the Trustees were looking at the possibility of going into partnership with Francis Noel-Baker, who owned a large estate in Euboea, the island north-east of Attica in Greece. The project was to encompass more than education, and reflected a renaissance of Dartington's preoccupation with rural revitalisation. Royston Lambert saw Euboea as a possible 'social work base'.

For various reasons, the Greek project came to nothing, and Royston turned his attention to another possibility that had arisen in Sicily. Julian David, who had been teaching comparative religion at Dartington, had been living with his wife Yasmin and three children in the small village of Scopello in north-western Sicily. The Davids had fallen in love with the place, its powerful landscape, and what Julian later described as the "moral beauty of the peasant culture". Scopello, with around 60 inhabitants was, in material terms and by English standards, very poor. Yet its subsistence culture remained rich in other ways and was relatively untouched by the mixed blessings of modern life. Though the Mafia was very much in control and had ear-marked the nearby coastal area for future tourist development, life in Scopello in the early 1970s presented a picture that had hardly changed for centuries.

Royston Lambert responded enthusiastically to Julian David's suggestion that Scopello should become the School's 'social work base abroad'. The Davids seemed well-established in the village and popular with its inhabitants. Lambert was aware that a similar project, run by Danilo Dolci and involving young volunteers from various European countries, was already in operation, and there appeared to be the possibility of working with them.

As far as Julian David was concerned, the project had two central aims: to help the local Sicilians, and to provide the ex-students from Dartington with an "experience that would blow their minds." There was an element of 1960s romance about the project, with distant echoes of the extended family base of Tagore's Santiniketan and the Elmhirsts' early Dartington. The David family would provide a central focus for the group, who would live communally while they learned at first-hand, and by 'doing', about the uncomplicated and ritualised life of the Sicilian villages. There were even hopes, at one time, that Scopello and the Davids' farm at Luscombe near Dartington might develop into twinned self-sufficiency projects with Luscombe acting as a training-ground for those about to set off to Sicily.

61

The Project was launched, paradoxically, by the time Royston
Lambert's honeymoon period at Dartington had reached its
waning phase. The more conservative Trustees were beginning
to react against his radical programme, and the scale of unchecked overspending caused by his energetic and expansionist
programme was beginning to cause alarm. Lambert gave the
go-ahead for the Project on the assumption that the Dartington
Hall Trustees would back it financially — but the support was
not forthcoming.

For the three years that it was in operation, (1971–73), the
Sicily Project survived on minimal funds: the School covered
Julian's salary, and parents contributed £5 a week for each
student, which was hardly sufficient, and the Project had to
raise funds by organising sales around Dartington. This penury
had beneficial side-effects: it provided a contrast to the privi-
leges of a private school, and lessened the gap between the
group's and the Sicilians' own level of subsistence.

Participation in the project was divided into two periods:
three months of training in England, followed by six months in
Sicily. In the 3-month preparatory period, Julian, Pat Kitto, and
Bernard Forrester (all previously teachers at Dartington Hall
School) set as their main task teaching the rudiments of Italian
language, some history, sociology and culture of Sicily, and a
taste of basic skills, including first aid, driving, cooking, youth
and social work, drama, pottery and other crafts, music, gardening and agriculture. With only three months at their dis-
posal, the group were only superficially prepared for taking
part in a 'social work' project.

The Davids themselves did not pretend to be anything other
than amateurs. It is easy enough to look back at the Sicily Project
and to wonder at the lack of professionalism which characterised
it, but such a perspective overlooks the actual spirit in which the
Davids hoped to work: there were no grand ambitions about 'aid'
or 'development', and the Project was seen as a modest beginning,
which would undoubtedly be of greatest 'learning'-value to the
English contingent, with possible benefit to the Sicilians as well.

The first group arrived in Scopello in January, 1971. They
lived with the Davids and their three children in relatively

primitive conditions. During the next six months, the various members of the group worked in a number of different ways: some stayed in Scopello where they helped the villagers with carpentry, house repairs, and in the fields. Others worked in local schools, offering simple arts and crafts activities which were not supplied within the Italian school system.

The idea of setting up a pottery in Scopello, with a view to encouraging local work, had always been central to the Sicily Project and the group received some training from Bernard Forrester, the pottery teacher at Dartington. The building of the kiln had to proceed by trial and error. The first pots were fired in April of 1971, four months after the arrival in Scopello. A new and more efficient kiln was built in the following year.

The young people set up a pottery project in a school for maladjusted and educationally sub-normal boys at Valderice, and made contact with Danilo Dolci. These did not turn out as well as had originally been expected, for the style of the two groups was radically different. Moreover, when Royston Lambert and Dolci met, their strong personalities clashed, and the Dartington group only ran a minimal number of craft courses at Dolci's centre. The connection with Dolci, who was openly fighting the control of the Mafia, did not help Julian in Scopello, and the association awoke suspicion.

Julian had expected that the Sicilian experience would 'blow a few minds', and Scopello, with its relatively untouched traditions must have initially struck the group as very exotic. And, indeed, acclimatisation to a fundamentally different set of values — so different in its strong social codes and its sense of honour, from the explosively libertarian atmosphere of the British early 70s — did not happen easily. Julian found that in this situation he had to assert a central focus of authority — which was almost as unfamiliar to the Dartington students as was the Catholic morality of the Sicilians.

Scopello, with its almost claustrophobic feel, provided one pole of the Sicily Project. Palermo, the island's capital, with its labyrinthine urban slums, provided the other. Several members of the group gravitated towards the city, 80 miles away from Scopello, where they practised a kind of ad hoc social work, linked to a number of other community education projects including a school for underprivileged children run by Tea Gallo. To an excessively critical eye, the struggles of the Sicily Project members who worked in Palermo, must have appeared close to hopeless: at one point, two of them were teaching a group of illiterate children to read and write — but with hardly any Italian, let alone Sicilian dialect. The conditions in which the Palermo group lived were very difficult, and the young people operated with minimal and geographically-distant support from Julian and the others. The Palermo connection was maintained throughout the three years of the Project. Just how much the local children benefited is hard to say, but probably not a great deal. It is unlikely that any harm was done, however, and there is no doubt that the experience was valuable for those members of the English group who chose to live and work in Palermo.

The first group of seven left Scopello in July 1971. The six months had been enormously rich, and they all emerged with much greater self-confidence. As in Yorkshire, the time in Sicily offered a context for initiation into an adult sense of social responsibility and choice. The group had established reasonable relations with the villagers, and by the summer of 1971, Julian had managed to set up a Scopello co-operative — with the approval of the Mafia — which was later to buy a communal tractor. This was no small achievement, considering that Julian was a foreigner, and that the group as a whole must have at times appeared threatening to the village.

Relations with Dartington, however, were not as good: although reports were sent back regularly to England, the Sicily Project suffered from its geographical and cultural isolation. The Project had an unavoidably separate existence from the School. There was a sense in which being in a very different world from South Devon was beneficial, as Sicily offered the chance for the young people involved to experience something radically different from the inwardness and exclusivity of Dartington Hall School. The distance, however, was a more negative consideration from the point of view of those left behind, for the School itself was hardly touched by the world of

Scopello. Though the possibility of such an adventure after 'A' levels may have attracted some prospective parents, beyond the Project's marketing value there was little in the way of serious or useful contact with Dartington.

In the second year, the Sicily Project focused much more on Scopello itself, although activities beyond it continued. A craft initiative involving young people in the neighbouring village of Castellamare was particularly well received by the local population. In Scopello, the carpenters in the group offered a free furniture-making and repair service to the villagers, and others helped regularly with agricultural work. The young women in the group had problems adapting to Sicilian sexual mores, and Julian and Yasmin had great difficulty in tempering the romances that flared up soon after the group's arrival in the winter.

By the summer of 1972, there was pressure from the local police for the group to move out. It was never clear whether this originated from the group's enemies in the village or the Mafia, who were involved in the tourist development of the coast near Scopello. Julian David was eventually able to secure the continuation of the Project for the following year, but difficulties increased. It was clear by this stage that the Dartington Hall Trust was not willing to help with consolidating the work in Scopello. Julian, who was very impressed by the Sicilian villagers' natural aptitude for craftwork and design, had wanted to raise money for the purchase of knitting machines, but the climate at Dartington was not favourable to such a development. Economic crisis, together with the growing tide of opposition to Royston Lambert's innovations, which came increasingly to be seen as extravagances, were contributory factors. The Sicily Project no longer had many allies at Dartington. At such a time of retrenchment, Dartington's priorities were changing: solvency and the need to stop the businesses losing money had become more important than experiment and adventure, which were draining away resources, even if on a relatively small scale.

The final year of the Sicily Project was coloured by a severe loss of commitment and enthusiasm on all sides. By the second year, the Davids had encountered difficulties with the group's observance of local taboos. In 1973, the group were no longer as willing to make allowances for Sicilian custom: some behaved like tourists, and drug-taking exacerbated the cultural distance between the Project and villagers, as well as driving a wedge between the Davids and the group. The last year, however, was not entirely disastrous, and the group built a new pottery that is still in use today. It was also in 1973 that the co-operative, whose birth Julian had facilitated, bought its tractor.

LOOKING BACK, over a decade later, it is difficult not to feel that the Sicily Project had, from the outset, been doomed to a short life. Of all Royston Lambert's ideas, the 'social work base abroad' was, by definition, the most difficult to run, control, and justify — particularly to those who could not easily imagine how rich such an experience might be for a young person on the threshold of adulthood. The Project both benefited and suffered from being low-key and unprofessional. It was also consistently under-funded, and it is arguable that an excellent opportunity was never given the chance it deserved. As an extension of 'school' into the world, and as a point of contact with traditional peasant culture, it was a remarkable experiment, unique and well ahead of its time. As Oliver Tringham, one of the second-year group, wrote in a later report, the Project offered the possibility of a "gentle birth out of the Foxhole womb, compared with the usual forceps delivering into university or tech."

The Sicily Project was swept into being on a wave of late 1960s enthusiasm; it is that same idealism, focused too single-mindedly on the positive possibilities of change, which carried within it the inevitability of the Project's lifespan being a short one. While the Sicily Project very faintly echoed the work that Leonard Elmhirst and Tagore had done in Santiniketan, it represented, on one level, a diversion from the business of strengthening the home estate. The Yorkshire Project, for all its positive qualities, was similarly diversionary.

The ROSLA Scheme, because of its link with Northcliffe, the local school, and because it was playing a role which the community recognised as essential, represented a pioneering move towards strengthening the bonds that arise from a shared sense of place. Yet Dartington, in reaching outwards, for many laudable reasons, was withdrawing energy and resources that might have been well used otherwise, considering the omnipresent threats of disintegration on the home front. Sicily and Yorkshire both embodied aspects of the radical vision that had fuelled the Dartington experiment, but by moving beyond the Estate before Dartington itself had been reintegrated, the two ventures were bound to lack much support from the centre, beyond the initial enthusiasm traditionally expressed for anything new and sufficiently attuned to Dartington's underlying preoccupations.

The central problem with Royston Lambert's plans for an 'anti-school' and the de-construction of educational institutions arose from the fact that they did not attach enough importance to those elements of the Dartington context which might have provided a 'heart' for the whole scheme.

Royston Lambert, for all the imagination of his ideas, was not a 'Dartington man' but an outsider, who could not be expected to feel the essential needs of the Estate and School — needs which were rooted in the particulars of Dartington's history, and which could only very partially be understood in terms of Lambert's somewhat ideological perspective. As with a number of other experiments at Dartington, the Sicily and Yorkshire ventures represented attempts at escaping the Estate's frustratingly parochial inertia: a human-scaled rhythm which is nevertheless central to the cultivation and survival of community.

From another point of view — and for this Royston Lambert was in large part responsible — these two projects, by taking Dartington outwards, kept Dartington in touch with the world beyond its boundaries, providing a necessary antidote to the inevitable isolation of the Estate. When Maurice Ash became Chairman of the Trust a few years later, he was quick to recognise the need to foster an equilibrium between

Dartington's needs as a community rooted in its own place and history, and the need to engage with the wider world.

The ROSLA Scheme at Conisbrough and the Sicily Project — although neither was intrinsic to Dartington's own development as an integrated Estate — were the forerunners of later educational ventures at Dartington (particularly the Work Experience and Postern Programmes) that explored a learning style which emphasised 'process' rather than 'product'. Rather than providing a package of facts, and institutionally validated qualifications, these projects stretched and enriched the young people who took part in them. In a sense that schools, colleges and universities seem to find almost impossible to assess and validate, the ROSLA Scheme and Sicily Project had undoubtedly helped to equip them for life.

IMPRESSIONS OF SICILY

*I*N *JUNE, 1971, Trustee Maurice Ash (later Chairman of the Trust) made a visit to Sicily. On his return he wrote the following impressionistic article for Dartington Hall News, Dartington's weekly newspaper.*

Wednesday.

It being already six in the evening, Julian took me straight from the airport into Palermo, to the school in the Piazza Marina. (If the traffic is anything to go by, Palermo is anarchy.) The Piazza Marina lies back of some quays and, parking the car there, to get to the school one walks into the slums: the blackened stone tenements of the old inner city.

Up a steep narrow stair, the school occupies some five rooms on the first floor. In most of these today little was happening, but in the furthest and smallest room there was a scene of ordered chaos: chaos, chiefly because of the noise from a dozen or more urchins in a confined space, some 12 feet by 6: ordered, because these children were mostly seated on benches around the wall, behind narrow tables, calling for their lessons like chicks for food. There (the centres of all this attention) were Rosemary and Steve. Beyond, in a still smaller room with the door shut, Tim was giving individual tuition to one child.

Into this scene, youths and young men — ex pupils — would wander, perhaps would take up a book and read for a few moments, or cuff the urchins into momentary silence. The urchins themselves would come and go at speed, as they wished. Yet learning was palpably taking place. The class lasts about an hour and a half, every weekday evening: no holidays. The pupils, mostly, are refugees from the official education system: a sort of ragged school. No girls: a male enclave.

Above the school, up a yet narrower stair to an attic, is a cupboard about 8 feet by 8 feet where Tim and Steve live throughout the week. Two camp beds: the small window blocked by wood against intruders: a gas ring. Comparison with the provision thought essential for sixth-formers at the Postern [Dartington Hall School's sixth form residential unit] came inevitably to mind.

Class over, we walk through the market that winds through the slums, now bright with lights against the sombre buildings and all animation. Many people affectionately greet our party, Julian especially. The looks cast on Rosemary, however, are predatory: she, inured to them, is composed and unconcerned. We have supper on a balcony above the centre of the market, walk the boys home (through some streets of unimaginable squalor), and take Rosemary, who is to return to Scopello with us, to collect her things from the pleasant middle-class family with which she lodges. She obviously has a life of her own within this family, embracing its several domestic dramas.

On the way home to Scopello, some 35 miles away, we call in at Dolci's centre, the Burgo. It is nearly deserted — apparently, as always. I begin to sense the distaste our young people have for it. For Rosemary, the famous mural about the Mafia is as sick with hate as the society it scoriates. I reserve judgement. We arrive in Scopello at about one in the morning, where Yasmin David is anxiously awaiting us alone by the fountain in the square.

Thursday.

I waken late in my 'pensione' — a house which, somewhat to my shame, has been reached by modern plumbing: apparently the only case yet in the village. I visit the Davids' lodging, up a rickety stair on the first floor of a peasant's house (the head of the family himself having this year finally emigrated in despair to America, at the age of 55). The Davids' living space is largely given over to a long table and benches at which Yasmin feeds the whole group. Entirely simple. I am lost to the enchantment of the David children. (These children have incidentally been very important for our young people: a contact with life from which their own age-group ironically has insulated them.) Close by, in a village of only some 200 souls, is the house where the group lives.

In a real sense, the group is assimilated into the village. They live in a peasant's house, draughty and leaky, almost without windows, and primitively crowded together. (The boys, much more domesticated than the girls — shades of the Army, for me: the girls' room, a more self-confident disorder.) But one half of the house, where I found them all working, is a space given over to crafts — pottery, jewellery, dress-making, carpentry. It is a high room, generous in dimensions, opening to the street. It is a social centre for the whole village — children, men and women — and it is good to see the comings and goings and the affection underlying this. The facility of our group in Italian is notable to me.

The girls have been taking their crafts into local schools and are eager to show me those few examples of their pupils' work in which some freedom of form and decoration has been expressed: a singular triumph in this rigid society. The girls' own pottery is modest, but they know it.

I find the group, personally, delightful to be with. Julian had told me how all had flowered, and so it seemed. They have lost nothing and gained much. In conforming to the village (only Tracy retains a touch of gypsy about her: but why not?) they have remained open and free as people: a sort of magic, which Royston is now trying to contrive at Dartington but to which I suspect Sicily more probably holds the key. Also, they have experienced and enjoyed the solidarity of a group, as otherwise they might never have done, and have done so in positive circumstances.

Julian takes me up the stoney valley behind the village where all the cultivated land lies, away from the steep fall to the sea, and where our group has its own plot of land. I am bitten by a dog outside a contadini's house, but this gains me admittance. Not so much a house, as a work-place: some decorated basket-work, high on one wall, the only sign of anything other than bare necessity. His plot is of perhaps ten acres: tomatoes, vines, egg-plants, barley. Immaculate. A mule and a cow their other possessions. One young son still there; the others have perforce left. The last working farmer in the valley. Julian hopes to make a co-operative on all this half-abandoned valley: to retain the identity of Scopello. He alone might do it. He is loved and respected — and, above all, detached from all their internecine suspicions. Our own plot, for which Bill is primarily responsible, is small (perhaps half an acre) but grows a variety of vegetable crops for home consumption. Julian is particularly concerned to experiment with sweet corn, hoping to ensilage this if his co-operative should materialise.

Lunch at the Davids: the only vegetarian meal I've ever enjoyed — perhaps because it's provided of necessity, not from moral conviction. From conversation, it emerges plainly that a merit of the whole experience to these young people is the very distance it affords them from which to evaluate life in Britain. This leaves them very ambivalent — but the experience is intensely educational.

In the evening I entertain everyone to dinner at the 'pensione' — a chance to eat some (scrawny) meat, for which some of them, not least the Davids' children, crave. They are intimate with the proprietor's family, and it is touching to see how an italianate sensuality of manner has superseded anglo-saxon frigidities. Fiona is a young woman now: companiable, balanced. Katrina retains her statuesque, quizzical quality, but that has subtlely been humanised. Bill's innate quietness has gained in assurance. And so on.

Friday.
Julian is to take Fiona and myself to Palermo, dropping Tracy on the way to fire some pots in the electric kiln at the Burgo. I endure the indigenous and incredible Italian bureaucracy, to change some money at the bank in Castellamare. We make a detour to the dour town of Alcamo, where the girls have taught crafts. Holidays there now, but the headmistress and a few children are present: she, a strong supporter of ours, but herself under duress to conform to the norms. Enough of an impression of this grim institution for my respect to grow for what our girls have pioneered. At the Burgo all is (typically) under lock and key and deserted. We leave Tracy to suffer alone the aridity of the place during many hours. Is there not something deeply misconceived about it?

Picking up Tim and Steve in Palermo, we first buy our lunch in the slum market and eat it free of charge at tables in a workman's restaurant. A sort of urban picnic: but really an instance of mutual help amongst the poor. Then, Tim directing the mini-bus with the unostentatious competence I now associate with him, we scour the slums for pupils. Out of this urban desert we gather about ten exuberant characters and take them up Monte Maggiore, high above Palermo. We play football on the asphalt car park at the windy top — and one, Matteo, excelling. On the mountain, we visit the shrine of Santa Rosalia, protectress of Palermo. At the entrance to the shrine, the urchins kneel frantically crossing themselves, looking scandalised as we walk indifferently past. Once within, however, they get out of hand and we beat a tactful retreat. They cling to one, and seem themselves not to know the difference between begging (for an ice cream: money for holy beads) and only asking for affection.

We descend to the city and to school. More children are at the door. I can only watch fascinated as Tim, Fiona, Steve and Julian conduct some two hours of riotous anti-school. All sorts of personal dramas were played out in this time, of different forms of attention-seeking. Fiona, for instance, has one boy alone, almost throughout the period, who had expressed a desire only for female tuition. His quiet dedication contrasted ironically with the crude treatment she had in general had to endure from the party that afternoon. Tim's perseverance in getting through to his wayward charges also moves me.

When it was over, Tim and Steve packed their camp beds and we started for Scopello. I reflected, there were some people at Dartington who had contended the Sicily group were evading reality. If it is with humanity itself such critics are concerned, perhaps they should themselves first experience the Palermo slums. As for the validity of the work the group is doing there, I think this stems from their very detachment: their credibility actually rests on their disinterest upon · a social (not personal) plane. At all events, I found it all deeply moving, indeed almost incredible.

Before returning, we sought out the benefactress of the whole school (one, Tea Gallo: a remarkable person, now desperately ill). She readily volunteered to accommodate Tracy and Katrina, who for the next two weeks also wished to work in Palermo. Having stopped at a familiar 'pizzeria' for supper on the way home, however, we were over an hour late in picking up Tracy. She was outraged at having been kept waiting in the desolate Burgo.

Saturday.
In the morning, I talked with Julian. I expressed my anxiety, that so much rested on him; he held so many delicate balances, that I feared for him and his family. He admitted the strain, the invasion of their family privacy. He had never imagined young people, so outwardly self-confident, would so much have need of him and Yasmin. Too much organisation also rests on Yasmin, who temperamentally prefers to do things herself. A different balance between boys and girls, as hoped for next year, should help. Perhaps, also, some different housing arrangements next year (if he can pull them off) will improve matters.

Julian remarked on the financial leanness of the whole exercise, positively welcoming this, and suggesting no resentment at the lack of Trustee backing. He worries about the future, but most particularly from the point of view of the reverse contact: of benefiting Sicilians at Dartington, particularly in relation to Dolci's new school at Partenico. He thinks a group at Scopello numbering 12 to 14 is the

73

optimum — next year there should be 10. Since this would be some 30% of any one year's leavers, the importance of the project for Dartington School itself can be inferred. There has been some embarrassment from visits by ex-Foxholers, quite insensitive to the local situation, though wanting to participate. This problem has to be worked out. It at least brings out the alternative to Scopello: a year of bumming around Europe. For some, this quite possibly is right; but for the group at Scopello, there's not much doubt which process is the more enriching.

Julian thinks the Mafia is very real, and growing, especially in the construction and development business. He admires Dolci for his refusal to compromise, but for himself he could not function that way nor, finally, would it accord with his view of life. This is yet one more balance he must hold, particularly for the sake of his all-important co-operative.

As for the feed-back factor, Julian sees this developing as the graduates of Scopello return to England. However, what he hopes for above all is the growth of a craft centre in connection with Dartington, such as might impart a sense of realism to the learning of pottery, textiles, etc., with a view to their application in Sicily. He hopes to retain the integrity of life he finds in Scopello as much through the practice of crafts (even though they are little practised now) as through the establishment of a viable agriculture.

Personally, I found Julian exceptionally impressive, whether observing his contact with people in the alleys of Palermo or in the village of Scopello. It is rare in my experience to find his spiritual quality in someone. We are unaware of how much he has taken upon himself, or of how central to the historical spirit of Dartington are his actions.

In the afternoon, Fiona, Rosemary, Katrina and Tim take me in the mini-bus to fill in my background of Sicily. The girls share the driving with Tim, and I marvel at their assurance on these difficult, dusty roads. We visit Erice on its conical, and all Sicily seems a garden at this moment of the year and continuously beautiful. In the evening we rendezvous with everyone else at Segesta. Excepting perhaps Delphi, I know no place with more of the atmosphere of classical Greece. Driving in convoy through the bewitching landscape, we finish with a twilight picnic (supplied abundantly by Yasmin) in a ghostly, abandoned manor, full of yesterday's sadness.

Sunday.
Every day my breakfast has mysteriously had to wait whilst they fetch the milk for my coffee. This time I follow the proprietor, pan in hand, as he goes to fetch it. Round the corner, down the street, he spies the goat waiting. He calls, she comes running, calling back, turns her rear to him and he pulls my milk. (She is called Monica.) The group shortly gather round my breakfast table to say good-bye, see butter there — so strange to them — and devour it. It is only two hours later, sitting in the airplane surrounded by harsh American and French voices, that I realise how great a chasm lies between the world I have been in and the one to which I am so casually returning.

It certainly makes one think.

Students and staff at The Postern, early 1980s.

CHAPTER FOUR

The Work Experience and Postern Programmes

D URING THE 1970s training became a key priority at Dartington: from horticulture and forestry at the beginning,
through to the Work Experience and Postern Programmes at
the close of the decade, the Trust devoted an increasing amount
of energy to projects which attempted to provide working
contexts for the acquisition of a wide variety of skills. As far as
Dartington was concerned this interest was not entirely new.
However, this time around it reflected a more widespread
cultural current; a growing sense of the need to make education
more relevant to the requirements of the work-place, as well as
providing a more adequate transition from school or college
into the world.

There was also, following the establishment of the North
Devon Project (which produced the Beaford Centre and the
glassworks at Torrington) and Royston Lambert's educational
ventures in Yorkshire and Sicily, a renewed interest in the
Estate. This represented a natural return to base — as part of
the rhythmic ebb and flow which has characterised the history
of Dartington since 1925 — as well as a response to gathering
national and local economic difficulties. This inward turn was
recognised and encouraged by Maurice Ash, who succeeded
Leonard Elmhirst as Chairman of the Trust in 1972. He saw this
as reaffirming the primacy of the Estate as a source of meaning
and identity for Dartington. Dartington's concern for 'vocational training' or 'work experience' did not just reflect a wish

to make education more relevant, but reflected also a concern for strengthening connections between the Estate's various constituent parts. The Estate's promise, as a place in which the process of reintegration might be fostered, was once again very strong.

During Royston Lambert's time as headmaster of the School, efforts had been made to bring together the various strands of 'vocational training' practised at Dartington. The horticultural and forestry training centres were seen by some as parts of Royston Lambert's vision of a de-constructed 'anti-school', and there were plans for an agricultural training centre as well. Such plans did not find much favour with established institutional interests and were not helped by the clash of strong personalities, and the scattering of Lambert's own energies in so many directions, including Yorkshire and Sicily. The general economic climate and Dartington's own financial problems did not help either. The idea of a multi-centered 'campus' survived Lambert's departure from the School in 1974 and continued to be discussed even after the Trust had withdrawn its support from the forestry and horticultural training programmes.

The aim to establish a coherent structure for vocational training was central to the period of Maurice Ash's Chairmanship of the Trust (1972–84). He referred, on many occasions, to the original purpose of the Estate as an educational resource: an idea which was, he believed, in the Elmhirsts' early days "ahead of its time and had collapsed for lack of understanding". The Work Experience and Postern Programmes are therefore to be understood in the light of these concerns as much as in the context of high unemployment and the government's various reactions to the problem.

Both programmes sought to make full use of the Estate as a 'classroom', making it possible for school-leavers, mostly from outside Dartington, to expand their horizons by working on a number of placements chosen from an exceptionally wide range of activities. The project also opened up Dartington's departments and enterprises in a way that brought staff into contact with young people's needs, and made them more directly aware of major social problems beyond the sheltered world of the Estate. In this way, the ordinary boundaries between school and work, young and old, were eroded, and the Estate gently nudged towards a measure of integration, as well as a greater understanding of Dartington's special identity.

During 1973/74, the government began to acknowledge structural and long-term unemployment. There was particular concern for youth unemployment and the growing chasm between traditional school-based education and the requirements of industry. The 1976 Special Measures Act, made funds available through the Manpower Services Commission (MSC) for the employment of school-leavers. The Act was primarily designed to tackle structural unemployment, but it provided Dartington with an opportunity to experiment further with finding ways of bridging the gap between school and work.

During the early 1970s, the ROSLA Scheme had demonstrated that there might be an alternative for those many school-leavers who went straight into inappropriate work or the dole queue. Youngsters often came out of school with a poor sense of their own worth, little initiative, and not much idea of what they wanted to do with their lives. Most of them had no experience of work, and were used to being told what to do and think by adults, be they parents or teachers. This scheme demonstrated that in a relatively short time, some of the damage inflicted in large impersonal schools could be repaired. The Terrace had pioneered a style of living, earning and learning which enabled youngsters to overcome a range of inner 'blocks'. This process involved handing over a great measure of responsibility to the young people, making them more aware of their power as individuals, their ability to choose for themselves, and the inevitable constraints which accompanied such freedom.

The experience of the Terrace and, to a lesser extent, of the horticultural and forestry training scheme on the home estate, had shown the Trustees and others at Dartington how the nurturing of individual choice, so essential to Dartington Hall School, could be extended beyond the sheltered enclosure of a fee-paying boarding school. When Dartington came to create a programme for school-leavers, this principle was as central to

79

the schemes as was the provision of work experience. It was indeed considered crucial to the transition from a childhood dependent on authority, into more responsible young adulthood.

When the Dartington Hall Trust approached the Manpower Services Commission in 1976 with a proposal for a Work Experience Programme, the plan was for something both unique and original. While many organisations were to exploit, to their own short-term advantage, the government's funds and the young people they were able to employ, or else to respond with limited imagination, Dartington used the opportunity to develop the idea which had been tried out with some success in Yorkshire, Sicily and the Estate's training centres. Roy Robinson, Director of the Programme and a former training director from GEC, described Dartington's brand of work experience to an MSC official as: "a time to experiment and mature while the pressure is off."

The Dartington programme was not just offering job experience and a constructive solution to unemployment, but: "the development of personal and social skills, awareness of personal capacity, and learning the responsibilities of adult working life". The scheme clearly embraced far more than work experience, as narrowly defined: it was an experiment concerned with tackling a problem that went much deeper than the unemployment figures which had stirred the government into action. The gap between school and work had steadily increased over a very long period — in fact, ever since schools started to become heavily institutionalised and classroom-based, concentrating on a predominantly academic style of learning. Not only did most British schools — unlike many of their counterparts on the Continent — fail to provide much in the way of practical or vocational education but, by virtue of institutional isolation and hierarchical organisation, they undermined the natural social processes which fostered development from dependent child into self-contained but responsible adult.

THE WORK EXPERIENCE PROGRAMME

T HIRTY THREE YOUNGSTERS, selected by the Careers Service, came on the first six-month programme. All were from the Torbay area, but ranged very widely in terms of academic achievement and social background. Many came from difficult homes. Candidates needed to have been substantially unemployed since leaving school, and were selected if it was felt that they would benefit from the scheme as a whole rather than because of their suitability for a particular job.

The Programme was jointly financed by the MSC and the Dartington Hall Trust, and the government body treated it as a special case as it was the only residential venture of its kind in the country. There were four programmes, running from Autumn 1976 until November 1978, at which point the Postern Programme was established and succeeded the Work Experience Programme. From the second programme onwards, the catchment area widened, to take special account of depressed rural areas beyond Torbay.

Some of the 'WEPs' — as the participants on the Programme soon came to be called — lived in digs and in the Gardens Hostel at Dartington, which had formerly been used by horticultural trainees. Most of the youngsters had never lived away from home or needed to cook for themselves. This aspect of the WEPs' experience was, for most, as important as anything else on the scheme. "Hostel life", wrote Peter McVae, one of the adults in charge, "is of vital importance ... From learning to be responsible through to catering for themselves and cleaning, there emerges a more self-sufficient and reliable youngster, determined to find and hold onto a job. This is also true of WEPs in digs, but the changes are greater and more noticeable in those who live together and support each other in a group environment."

The six-month period was divided into a number of 'placements', at least two of which were selected with a view to exposing the WEPs to jobs they did not especially want. The 'core placement' which was considerably longer, offered the youngsters a chance to work in the their chosen field. Jane

81

Perry, for example, who had left school with five CSEs had spent two weeks in the Trust's offices at Shinners Bridge, a week in the Cranks Restaurant at the Cider Press, two and a half months with the payroll office, followed by two months at Dartington Litho, a printing business operated by the Trust. Interviewed at the time, Jane told of how her confidence had been greatly increased during the six months. She had learned "not to rely on anybody else, to see if you could work things out for yourself." After the programme, Jane was taken on full-time at Dartington Litho. Les Hare, another youngster on the same programme, spent two weeks with the Trust's catering business, a week in one of its shops, and the remainder of his time at Dartington Hall Tweeds — which was then a Trust-owned operation. At the end of the six months, he was offered a job at the mill as a trainee weaver.

By the second programme (Easter to October 1977), placements included Dartington Hall Tweeds, Dartington Hall Farms, the Estate Department, Dartington Litho, the Gardens, Dartington Woodlands, Dartington Sawmills, Dartington Plant, the Dartington Social Research Unit, Dartington Hall Caterers, Dartington's various retail outlets, the various Trust Offices and Cranks Restaurant.

All the WEPs spent a week with Roy Robinson, the Programme Director, in which they developed job application skills. There was also a week at the Brathay Training Centre in the Lake District, where 'outward bound' techniques were used to develop the youngsters' self-confidence and initiative. Wherever possible, outside opportunities were used to broaden the group's experience. In June 1977, as a contribution to the Jubilee celebrations, the WEPs worked together for a day on the landscaped hillocks at the Cider Press's new car park, helping plant trees and bushes. The WEPs also acted as hosts and caterers for a number of social functions to which employers, MSC officials and others were invited. These occasions did not just stretch the young people, who had never had to entertain formally before; they also provided a unique context in which Dartington's usually disparate departments could meet. Contact between heads of department was otherwise limited to quarterly 'Liaison Committees', Foundation Day and a Christmas Buffet. The Work Experience Programme, by cutting across departmental boundaries, informally brought the various departments of Dartington together.

Initial reactions to the Programme from Dartington's executives and heads of departments varied. Some confessed to being suspicious of the Trust's 'latest enthusiasm'. But support soon grew and the WEPs found themselves, in the majority of cases, warmly adopted. Although it seemed likely that the Programme might suffer from some of the problems that had, fifty years earlier, plagued the original attempt to use the Estate as a 'classroom' (the Trust's various departments and companies were not, after all, set up with a view to training and offering placements), in general, the system seemed to work remarkably well. The general success of the project was largely due to the fact that it was run with energy and commitment, and with a sense of clarity and direction. Confidence in the project was boosted by a widespread and growing recognition of the needs of unemployed school-leavers. There is no doubt, however, that the value derived from placements, and the suitability of various activities to 'work experience' varied a great deal, and that some WEPs were bored and some others exploited as cheap labour.

It is difficult to make an overall assessment of the achievements of the Work Experience Programme at Dartington. Much of the value of the experience was subjective, and there could be no qualifying examination. However, between 75% and 80% of the WEPs found full-time employment at the end of their six-month programme, which gives some measure at least of the Programme's efficacy in relation to employment. The Programme also played its part in nurturing the perennial image of an integrated Estate: a setting in which caring could be explored collectively. The WEPs, in fact, more than any others at Dartington, were allied to the Estate *as a whole*, and by their easy movement from placement to placement crossed boundaries that ordinarily seemed impermeable.

'BACK TO OUR ROOTS'

M AURICE ASH,Chairman of the Dartington Hall Trust from 1973 to 1984 has always been a quietly passionate advocate of 'the Estate as a classroom'. In the 1977 edition of Dartington's Annual Report, he contributed the following introduction to a special section on the Work Experience Programme.

Sometimes people will say — and they probably think it more often than they say it — that Dartington may be all very well, but it's not part of the real world. I'm tempted to reply by asking which is 'real' — the world, or Dartington: by which I mean, which of the two is alive and has the future in it. But of course, that's not very helpful towards achieving any meeting of minds, and often it's better to stay silent and let actions speak louder than words.

Consequently, it's very gratifying to find Dartington doing something that makes sense to the world, and to be amongst the first to do it. Thus, our work experience programme would seem to prove to any doubters that Dartington knows and cares about what's real in the world: namely, the plight of the young unemployed.

Now, I hope this is the case, but people should also beware that things may not be quite as they seem. Dartington's participation in this scheme is in fact a realisation of the original purpose of the Estate. As such, it was a project we already had on the boil when the Government's scheme to mitigate the effects of unemployment provided us with the means to implement it. Had those means not become available, we should have sought others. In that event, one wonders, would people still have said Dartington was unreal?

For the idea of the Estate — now, as fifty years ago — is that it is an educational resource. When Dartington began, the Estate was the classroom of the School; there virtually was no other. The idea was ahead of its time and collapsed for lack of understanding. Our purpose has been to revive it, now that the Estate is so much richer in resources and that the understanding to make it happen has grown. Our work experience scheme is therefore fundamentally educational in kind.

Please don't think that this means the scheme is not to do with the real world. The idea of education we have in mind may not be

84

vocational in the narrow sense of the word. We are not involved in training, as such: in teaching specific skills — or not primarily so. Rather, the education in question is precisely that which Dartington has always preached and practised: growth of personality, of a person's ability to look after himself in the world. This is the educational purpose which the Estate is now once again serving, and the great difference between now and fifty years ago is that people want to share their knowledge with the young. I suspect they do so because to share it is to give so much more meaning to the knowledge one has.

If anyone thinks that to use a government scheme for the unemployed to serve an educational purpose is not quite playing the game, I would ask them to look at the results. A staggering proportion (80%) of our first intake had found jobs by the end of their allotted six months. And the reason they had done so is obvious. They had, quite simply, learnt to talk. And they had learnt to talk because they had grown in self-confidence. And they had grown in self-confidence because they had been treated as people. Thus, this very representative cross-section of thirty or so young people came to stand out from their contemporaries who, despite (or because of?) the spread of 'education' remain so strangely inarticulate. And if you are inarticulate you will find it hard to understand, and hence acquire, the skills you will need.

The moral I am tempted to draw from this is that Dartington seen as an educational community is more real than the world itself. However, there are good grounds for thinking that the world itself — or considerable parts of it — is quite in tune with our way of thinking. To start with, the Manpower Services Commission, under whose auspices our scheme is running, seems quite aware of the educational character of what it is attempting to do for young people up and down the country. And there would seem to be large and successful parts of British industry which are actually interested in the person, not in his theoretical qualifications. There are increasing areas of industrial training itself which are practising some kind of 'action learning'; which means, learning about yourself from what you are doing. And the only way to learn about work, after all, is by working. That is why we ourselves, at least, have concluded that work experience — or, as we now often call it, 'work education' — is a phase existing in its own right: neither work itself, nor school, but as essential as each of these and to be continued at all costs — outside the normal system, if necessary.

For school, this must mean that it is not a place for chasing futile qualifications. Parents' insecurity, surely, is what accounts for this, not the realities of life itself. School is for the child to grow, as the child he is. Thus our experience of earning and learning has served to endorse the idea of education that Dartington has always held. This idea of education is still a radical one, and always will be, because it starts with people — and people are so darned unpredictable. That's reality!

LEARNING TO LIVE WITH OTHERS

*L ESLEY CHAMBERLAIN a trainee on Dartington's Work Experi-
ence Programme in 1978, described her impressions in an
article which was published in WEP, an occasional xeroxed publication put together by the trainees.*

Community life is never easy at the best of times, except perhaps
when the interests and states of mind of the communards are
similar and unified. Even then, petty conflicts have been known to
arise, and even to destroy the staunchest of communes. So here
I am, living at the Gardens Hostel at Dartington, amongst people I
often cannot identify with, whose interests are not mine and
whose life-styles would dissatisfy me. We are all so different on
this particular Work Experience Scheme, the divisions between
us many, but somehow it all seems to work quite well. I was
afraid at first, when I met the other WEPs. There seemed some
rather strange people among them and I was unsure which sect
of them I belonged to. My first impulse was to be extremely
careful, not to criticize their musical tastes, speech or style of
dress, and somehow to dull my own personality for fear of total
rejection.

Happily, over a short time I grew used to everyone —
intolerant of them or pleased with their company as I was — and I
was surprised to find that acceptance came easily. The Gardens
Hostel itself is a pleasant building, certainly not grim or unhomely.
It is always slightly dirty and lived-in, but the dirt is not filth, it is
more a fine dust that lays over everything and is never quite
removed even after the most avid cleaning operation. We are
very young people, most of us fresh from living at home where
the odd plate you left lying around would be picked up by your
mother; it isn't easy to conform so suddenly and become house-
proud. Activities within the hostel are limited. Luckily we have a
colour TV, and there are a few record players scattered around,
owned by various WEPs. ('WEPs' means us.)

I consider myself one of the lucky ones, because the short-
term jobs I have so far done on this course have been so totally
different from each other, therefore opening many doors for me
with regards to my career. I am unsure exactly what I want to do
with my life, but it is good to know that I have had a wide range of
jobs that may well help me to get into long-term employment.

My first work experience was working in the box office at Dartington Hall, lending me useful information about office work. I then moved to work for Peter Tysoe, the sculptor and glass blower, near Shinners Bridge. This I enjoyed immensely. My experience included tinning metals, learning how to cut basic glass shapes, and it finally gave me a chance to try my hand at glass engraving, something I have craved to do for a long time. This was the artistic side of my employment.

I was then moved to the Cider Press, to work in the glass shop and craft shop. I enjoyed this a great deal, and was given many helping hands by the rest of the staff, for which I was extremely grateful.

Roy Robinson's policy for me at the beginning of the course was to plunge me straight into an office, the total antithesis of my more 'arty-crafty' nature. And though I was quietly annoyed at first, I now realize how useful and necessary it was for me to move away from the one-track state of mind I had at the time (wanting to be an artist), and to discover whether or not I could work in an office away from other more desirable (artistic) surroundings. I found to my pleasure that I could, and even enjoyed myself during the time that I was there.

The course finishes in November. The months have passed quickly but fully for me. I feel that I have used my time so far to my own advantage. The course saved me from a stretch on the end of an unemployment queue and perhaps endless weeks of spiritual and physical laziness — something I can never afford to let happen again, as it did once before, when everything within and about me seemed to fall into a state of lethargy and uselessness.

I used, at the best of times, to be an intolerant centrepiece for myself. But this could not truly be maintained at the Gardens Hostel for very long, and though I wouldn't say this indulgent personality has been quelled at all, it has learnt to live amongst other young people who are totally unlike myself. Seclusion is not possible, you are not left alone for long with your own strange thoughts. There is too much noise and someone is usually knocking on your door wanting to talk or borrow something. This has been good for me. I feel slightly human at last, after a long lonely year of having no friends, no work, no money, and so little hope. It isn't good to be young and without hope; that was how some of us were at the beginning — I myself and the other WEPs — and it's all due to one scruffy little hostel, Roy and Fran, and enough marvellous employers situated throughout Dartington and Totnes who are willing to take us on and give us a chance.

It is a grim thought for me that for each one of us that have been given this chance, there are a hundredfold who have little or no hope and nothing to turn to.

THE POSTERN PROGRAMME

THE SUCCESS of the Work Experience Programme stimulated a re-examination of the Trust's educational goals on the Estate and beyond. The Programme had demonstrated Dartington's potential as a unique learning community and inspired a wave of enthusiasm for experimentation. Not surprisingly, this mood affected the School, which had experienced a period of retrenchment following Royston Lambert's departure.

The School's curriculum was in most respects conventional, and the general '16–19 year-old crisis' in education — raising so many issues concerning the transition between school and work — was considered by some to be as urgent a problem at Foxhole as anywhere else. There were all of a sudden plans for a new School, which would in some way encompass some of the spirit and practice of the Work Experience Programme. It was almost as if, in a matter of years, Royston Lambert's plans had been forgotten. A 'think-tank' was assembled and numerous proposals drawn up. Michael Campbell, then Head of English at the School, proposed an 'alternative educational community', which would offer, in the tradition of so many progressive experiments of the past, a model of 'the world as we would like it'. There would be no staff as such, only potters, horticulturalists, smallholders or others, and all involved would be committed to a revolution in lifestyle. Maurice Ash, the Trust's Chairman, echoing Leonard Elmhirst's words in 1925, wrote that "the school I am talking about ... is first of all an enterprise engaged with the world in various ways, and only secondarily a school." The enterprise would, above all, make the world meaningful to those who took part.

Perhaps not surprisingly, Campbell's idea proved too idealistic for the School and the Trust, although some ideas from this proposal, including goats, chicken and a vegetable garden, did reappear in the Postern Programme. The Trust had hoped that the Work Experience Programme might, by integration within the School, radically alter the nature of the education of sixth-formers at Foxhole. Maurice Ash and others hoped that the institutionalisation of the School, as a separate community on

90

the Estate, which went back to W. B. Curry's appointment as head in 1931, might be reversed. But institutions breed perspectives, values and practices that are not easily changed; and although Roy Robinson's offices were located at Foxhole, the 'styles' of Dartington Hall School and the Work Experience Programme were in many ways very different.

When the Postern Programme was finally established it was presented as a "joint venture between Dartington Hall School and the unique residential Work Experience Scheme which was supported by the MSC and Dartington Hall Trust". In reality, however, the School and the Postern Programme worked as distinct organisations, although there was a measure of mutual overlap. The Postern Programme represented, first and foremost, an expansion of work experience to include not just unemployed school-leavers but others who had stayed on at the School during the sixth form but wanted a break, or who wished to maximise the use of time between school and higher education. Although the Programme was to make use of Foxhole facilities and staff, the Postern's impact on the School itself was minimal.

The Postern Programme started in October, 1979, just six months after the close of the Work Experience Programme. Thirty-five 'Posterners' came from Devon and were supported, as the WEPs had been, by the MSC under the Youth Opportunities Programme. Twenty to twenty-five others came from all over the UK and from overseas, on a fee-paying basis. While the MSC group were 16–19 year-olds, the 'private' group ranged from 15–22 year-olds. The Programme's organisers were keen to make every effort to maintain as much of a mix as possible "in terms of social, academic and economic backgrounds, as well as career aspirations, sex, personality, and physical capabilities".

The staff consisted of Roy Robinson (Director), Geoff Dowson (Placements), Sue Chapman (House Manager) and Stuart Lindeman (Educational Director). There were also four volunteer hostel advisers, who received free board and accommodation, and lived in the residential blocks. The advisers also helped with leisure activities and pastoral care. The Programme was financed by the Dartington Hall Trust and MSC, as well as by parents' fees in the case of 'private' students. Each Posterner received a weekly 'wage', which was drawn from fees or from the MSC's per capita grants.

The Programme was described in the original prospectus as a "new bridge between school and life", and as an "exit from school which is also an entry into life". There were echoes of the ROSLA Scheme in Yorkshire, the Sicily Project, and naturally the Work Experience Programme. This time, the issues of structural unemployment and rapid technological change were presented as unequivocal reasons for offering an educational experience which would enable youngsters to survive in a world which would not necessarily owe them a secure living. Such a world would require initiative, self-reliance and confidence, just as much as academic qualification. In the Postern's brochure, the Programme was presented as offering a space in which young people could work out their own ideas about their future. Under the banner of 'Living, Learning, Earning', the project combined "work experience, individual development and social living". The course structure was unique, though strongly influenced by previous Dartington experience.

The 'programme' for each individual lasted 26 weeks, but fee-payers could stay longer, as could some special MSC cases. The first 21 weeks of the course were devoted to work placements, followed by specialisation in a chosen field of work. As with the Work Experience Programme, the purpose behind the placements was not primarily to give Posterners specific skills or knowledge that might help them in their subsequent careers but, in the words of the Programme brochure, "to help the participants come to terms with new experiences and to assess them for themselves." Posterners' preferences were taken into account when organising placements, but the organisers stressed the value that many youngsters might derive from persevering in a job that at first seemed boring or inappropriate.

About 70 businesses, many of them off the Dartington Estate, participated in the scheme, and a range of over 200 types of work was offered. These included most of the areas that had been open to the WEPs, with the addition of a large number of outside enterprises, including kennel and stable work, building trades, engineering, fish farming and others. In the summer, the Posterners ran a small business selling cream teas to visitors. Other small business enterprises included the running of a small market stall in Totnes.

Catering and housekeeping at the Old Postern itself — the former medieval parsonage and the adjoining modern hostels that had most recently housed the School's sixth-form section — provided a work placement. There were also goats, ducks and chickens, which were looked after by the Posterners and supplied produce for the kitchen. The Postern employed two experienced kitchen workers, but no maintenance or cleaning staff.

Generally speaking, the placements worked well. A small number of Posterners could not cope with the disciplines of time-keeping, hard work, and work that was sometimes boring. A few of these, and others who could not adapt to community life, were asked to leave. Employers were asked to write reports on Posterners at the end of each placement. About two-thirds of the fifty employers involved in the first programme were sufficiently satisfied with the Posterner placed with them to note that they would be prepared to employ them if a job became available. While in the earlier part of the six-month period, employers wrote of "slowness, shyness and lack of self-confidence", there was a marked change by the end of each programme, with the Posterners becoming markedly more sure of themselves.

In addition to placements, the Posterners took part in five 'work release courses', each lasting one week. These covered 'induction', 'work environment', 'communication', 'personal development' and 'job and further education interviews and applications'. The approach to these courses was experiential, and involved participatory exercises, simulations, role-play, action research, drama, video and games. There were also visiting speakers, films, and outside visits.

The theme of 'personal development' was central to the entire programme. Every opportunity was taken to strengthen each Posterner's sense of self-awareness, and this involved a recognition by each individual of his or her strengths as well as limitations. Activities such as rock climbing, caving, canoeing, and night navigation on Dartmoor, provided specific challenges to the group and a chance for individuals to test themselves, and subsequently to reflect upon their reactions to a demanding experience. Each activity, whether 'outward-' or Old Postern-bound, was followed by group discussion, as the process of reflection was considered essential to the Postern's particular form of learning by doing.

The staff involved the Posterners as much as possible in the planning of course activities. The same principle applied to the organisation of daily life in the Old Postern buildings, and every Friday afternoon, the group met to discuss the 'business of the community'. The meetings were always chaired by a Posterner, and the agenda drawn up by the group. The rest of the afternoon was designed "to bring the week to an end in a meaningful way", and also to make a connection between the content of the 'course weeks' and their work experience. Activities included 'course options' such as drama, art, photography, or producing a magazine; a group discussion in which Posterners talked about their experiences at work; and the 'pay session', at which each young person was paid his or her weekly 'wage'.

Posterners who wished to pursue academic work could take examinations. In one year, around 20 out of 60 Posterners might be sitting for GCEs or CSEs — most of these MSC-sponsored. In some cases they joined classes at Dartington Hall School, but arrangements were also made for individual tutoring. Contact with the School was limited in most cases to sports, and to joint classroom and outdoor activities. The two communities were, inevitably, distinct, with different rhythms, attitudes and goals. However outward-looking the Postern might have been, the Programme's emphasis on working intensively as a group tended to make reaching out difficult, except when common ventures made practical sense, such as in making up a football or rock-climbing team.

While both organisations shared aspects of a common heritage, the Postern had moved boldly beyond the world of

'school' or 'college'. The School did emphasize individual development, but much of the week was still spent in the pursuit of
abstract knowledge and, ultimately, exam qualifications. The
Postern, without sacrificing discipline and structure, was a
place in which process was valued as highly as product. By
aiming "to help people become self-sufficient in the fullest
possible way", the Programme was committed to nurturing
subtle changes in each person, and to an open-ended and
individually responsive series of events. The Postern differed
from the School in that it did not cultivate personal development in isolation from work and relationships to other people.
As the Education Director, Stuart Lindeman put it: "At the
Postern, we developed self-sufficiency in a number of ways
that were inter-related and grounded upon the experience of
work."

As had been found with the ROSLA Scheme at Conisbrough
(which Stuart had been involved with in its final year) most
school-leavers were unable to take responsibility for themselves, and were not prepared for the demands of adult life
even if they had done well academically. Every aspect of the
Postern Programme was seen as playing a part in developing
for each student a sense of self, both personally and in relation
to other people. The MSC distinguished between various 'life
and social skills', which they described in terms of a package of
'process competences' which could be taught. These were iden-
tified as "communication, planning, the ability to think logi-
cally, the analysis of information, clear and accurate writing ..."
etc. The Postern used the official terminology but applied the
idea more radically, moving beyond a definition which reduced
self-determination and self-awareness to a series of definable
skills. This was achieved by consciously breaking down the
divisions between 'work' and 'personal development', and
thinking of the whole Postern process as a continuum of
inter-related experiences.

The Postern Programme ran from October 1979 until September 1983. It was closed down as a result of a change of government
and MSC policy and with the establishment of the Youth Training
Schemes (YTS). The Postern had always been treated as a 'special

case' with considerable support from the MSC in the South West, but under YTS its exceptional status could no longer be accommodated. The Pontin Charitable Trust, an associated charity, had under-written the venture in its early stages and Dartington had, throughout, covered any Postern deficits.

It seems particularly tragic that the Postern Programme had to be discontinued for lack of government funding rather than inherent failings. In its two years of operation there is no question that the Programme's formula had proved itself, while responding to a demand that seemed to be growing rather than shrinking. The Postern was particularly remarkable because it was able to tread new ground adventurously, yet within MSC guidelines, whilst so many ventures which have been made possible through skilful use of government support have lacked imagination. The Postern was a unique experiment, not least because it combined fee-payers and MSC-backed students.

Joint ventures with government organisations, as the Trust had discovered with other collaborative ventures, have always been as risky as they are fruitful. Continuity can never be assured, as government policies — particularly in the field of youth unemployment — have been subject to the demands of expediency and electoral politics. There was a price to be paid for being creatively opportunistic: in the Postern's case, it meant the closure of a highly successful and original programme.

WITH THE CREATION of YTS, the Trust once again became involved with youth training based at the Postern, but this time under the aegis of the 'Dartington Tech' which was set up in 1983. Under a new 50-week scheme, open to 16–17 year old school-leavers, 'life and social skills' were treated much as they are in other parts of the country — in other words, with little direct relationship to day-to-day living or work. Although some work placements are organised at Dartington, and there are thirty or so short-term residential trainees at any given point in time, there is now no special relationship between the new Postern Training Agency's YTS Scheme and the Dartington

Estate, as there had been with the Postern Programme; and as YTS was not residential, the Scheme has not benefited from concentrated community-living. YTS offered, in many respects, a poor substitute for the initiation into self-awareness and adulthood which the Postern provided so well.

While the Tech's YTS Scheme could not reproduce the intimacy and strong focus of the Postern, it made possible the setting up of the South Devon Microcentre which offered young people a year's intensive and practical training in the use of small computers. The Microcentre was set up to operate as a small business, offering special courses for women and the handicapped. In 1985 a new Dartington Centre for Woodland Training (later called the Dartington Forestry Training Group) was opened, also under the sponsorship of Dartington Tech. Courses at the Centre were at the outset designed to train men and women to work competently in both unmanaged and commercial woodlands, and to be able to do so either on a directly employed or self-employed basis. The Dartington Tech's commitment to practically-based learning does, however, still reflect one important facet of the original ideas which launched the Dartington experiment.

THE POSTERN PROGRAMME originally grew out of the success of the Work Experience Programme but it had also been conceived, in part, as a response to continuing discussions within Dartington Hall School concerning the appropriateness of its curriculum to rapidly changing times. Although the Postern was separate from the School, its success undoubtedly influenced the School and reinforced a changing climate of ideas. A 'Link' scheme was devised by two Foxhole teachers, and represented a first attempt at changing the content of the School's education. 'Link', during the time it was in operation, offered students at the School a wide range of possibilities for extending their contact with the world. 'Link' activities included producing a newspaper, making a video, building work, the collection of edible plants, visits abroad, making jewellery, and many other non-academic activities.

While 'Link' represented an important step in the direction of more 'appropriate' learning — in most cases through doing — it nevertheless confined itself to specialised activities and did not touch upon the more general areas of self-reliance and social responsibility. Maintenance, cleaning, cooking, and the growing of produce were still supplied to a School population that expected to be serviced when it came to the most basic necessities. Neither did 'Link' open up much opportunity for contact between the School and the Estate, for the School's sense of itself had not fundamentally changed: the primary focus of attention remained the child, and such child-centeredness carried with it a refusal to engage directly with the priorities of a world in which the 'child', as conceived within the 'progressive' culture since Rousseau's time, could no longer be quite so central.

After John Wightwick's resignation as head, the Trustees and School Governors consciously sought a head who might take the School closer towards the kind of 'learning and living' that had been so successfully tested at the Postern. The tragic story of Lyn Blackshaw's short period in charge of the School, and the aftermath of disillusion and chaos, did not help change basic attitudes or the context in which 'Link' activities were pursued, however enthusiastic and committed individual members of staff might have been. The turmoil of the period and the misjudgements and misunderstandings that characterised it, may have been inevitable given the extent to which the School had become stuck within a framework of out-dated ideas and practices. The 'link' that was sought reflected a need for direct contact with realities beyond classroom and curriculum.

ALTHOUGH RELATIVELY SHORT-LIVED, the Work Experience and Postern Programmes made an essential contribution to Dartington. Both projects brought the Estate into close contact with social problems which the shelter offered by the Trust's status and resources might have otherwise enabled Dartington to ignore. But, apart from providing a human connection between Dartington's privileged and experimental world, the despair of the dole queue, and the constrained and bureaucratic thinking of the MSC, the two projects made an undeniable impact on the Estate itself. Both ventures made visible the totality and range of Dartington's many activities, in a way that no other enterprise, except the School in its earliest years, has ever done. As long as departments, companies and other projects continued to operate within the confines of a limited or specialised perspective, the vision of a coherent 'Dartington' remained little more than an ideal or a myth.

The two Programmes provided concrete evidence of a real Dartington community which was able, through the presence and movement of WEP's and Posterners, to recognise itself as a meaningful whole. The Work Experience and Postern Programmes did not just use the Estate 'as a classroom'; they brought vitality and a sense of identity to those who worked at Dartington. The practice of 'learning by doing', with its emphasis on active engagement, integrates rather than separates, and the WEPs and Posterners, in their involvement with the most widely recognized currency of the Estate — work — strengthened the threads of community.

By concerning themselves in a very practical way with a very concrete problem — the transition from School to work, and the need to initiate young people into self-awareness and a responsible and self-sufficient adulthood — the two projects avoided the detachment which can accompany the teaching of knowledge and skills abstracted from the flow and constraints of life. The groundedness of the approach was reinforced by the limited but real context of the Estate and its many activities.

The Dartington community cannot have been immune to the significance of the youngsters' initiation into the adult world. In providing a context for such a 'rite of passage', Dartington went some way towards 'adopting' the WEPs and Posterners, and it was hardly surprising that a number of them should eventually have been taken on as full-time employees, and as members of the Dartington 'family'. This caring role, which is essential to Dartington as a human-scale rural community, was strengthened by the presence of the WEPs and Posterners, and supplied a new source of vitality for the forces which have kept the

Estate from succumbing to the centrifugal pull of constant growth and innovation.

It was deeply revealing of Dartington's paradoxical relationship to the immediate locality, that *most* of the WEPs and Posterners merely 'passed through'. The two schemes, however involved with the Estate, were 'foreign' creations, catering to people who in the majority of cases had no previous or subsequent connection with the Estate. The Work Experience and Postern Programmes came closer than any other project at Dartington to realising the ideal of a 'learning community' which can initiate its young members without having to send them away or entrust them to a caste of professionals; but the two programmes were primarily directed at outsiders — which is symptomatic of Dartington's ambivalence about the task of reintegration.

The Work Experience and Postern Programmes were also important because they provided a tangible indication of how Dartington's perennial but hitherto conflicting concerns for 'individual space' and a 'living and learning community', might be combined. At the Postern, with its sophisticated educational philosophy and practice, the development of each person's self-awareness and confidence was treated as inseparable from the practical realities of the living community and work-place. The ability to make choices — a freedom which, somewhat paradoxically, raises issues of responsibility and relationship — was believed to be an inherent possibility within each person rather than an inalienable right. Such a potential for self-knowledge, it was believed, could only be fostered through interaction with others, and through the challenge of work disciplines and routine.

'Learning by doing', in this context, went far beyond the mere acquisition of skills. For it placed those skills in a context which encompassed more than a collection of individual lives. Self-realisation — a learning about oneself through experience — was not an isolated process, but arose out of contact with others and engagement with the working world. The sense of 'self' was inseparable from a relationship to 'place': a sense of identity and belonging. The Postern Programme, and the Work

Experience Programme to a lesser extent, made an essential connection between 'learning by doing' and a living and learning community. Learning, at the Postern, had to do with seeing and making relationship, a binding rather than a separating activity or process. A community which is alive to the 'patterns that connect', to use Gregory Bateson's phrase, will naturally tend towards a form of learning that comes from a 'doing' that is not divorced from the mainstream of life. In appreciating this, the Postern provided a much needed counter-balance to the emphasis on individual freedom and child-centeredness that had coloured Dartington Hall School since its early days.

REFLECTIONS ON THE POSTERN EXPERIENCE

*T*HE AUTHOR, *as editor of Dartington Voice, a quarterly community-based magazine, between 1981 and 1984, interviewed the Postern Programme staff. Five months after this interview the project was abandoned, primarily because of changes in government policy and the establishment of the 'Youth Training Scheme', which did not allow for special cases like the Postern. Those interviewed included Stuart Lindeman (Director of Education), Geoff Dowson (Work Placement Co-ordinator), Vanessa Harvey (Secretary and Administration), Sue Chapman (Catering and Domestic Co-ordinator), and Rachel Stevens (hostel adviser and recent university graduate).*

The team was characterised by its youth, enthusiasm and commitment. As their comments make clear, the Postern as a whole was a learning community with an unusually strong bond between trainees and staff.

The interview is followed by the results of a questionnaire to ex-Posterners, which was devised and administered by members of the Dartington Social Research Institute, an organisation which specialises in the study of the education and institutional care of young people, particularly young offenders.

Mark: First of all, what do you feel the purpose of the Postern has been: why somebody would come here instead of being on the dole for six months?

Sue: A lot of people on the dole don't seem to have any purpose in their life. It's just a humdrum sort of routine. To come here, it gives you a purpose. You've got a reason to get up in the morning and you've got a reason for meeting people, and for going out and about and getting to know people. You've instantly got six months of purpose and then a board to spring off to other things. You make people aware of what they can do and aware of their abilities: you make them feel important again. Because on the dole you don't feel very important; you don't feel as if you're doing anything for anybody.

Stuart: And it's interesting which side you look at it from. If the MSC were to say what's successful about the Postern Programme they would express it in terms of having to get a job, but in many cases we don't look at it like that at all. It's very much to do with how much people have developed inside themselves. Having been through the educational system and social pressures which don't allow people to sort things out themselves or to take responsibility, what we try to do in the six months is set up situations where they can take some responsibility; where they can make some decisions.

Mark: How would you describe your working style at the Postern?

Stuart: For me it's very much a counselling approach: not to make any decisions for the other person; not to give any particular advice about what they must do with their lives, but simply allow them to look at themselves more clearly and give them the opportunity to try different things out and look at the alternatives open to them. And during the six months of the programme, that's where the real development comes from. This kind of approach is lacking everywhere you see around you.

Vanessa: I think one of the things that comes over to me is that the kids come here thinking that it's an escape and that it's going to be totally different — all the things that Mum and Dad have told them that they should be doing or shouldn't be doing and all the things that teachers have told them. Being here for six months teaches them that it's no different from out there: everything's the same. If you come here and you throw your Coca-Cola cans through the hall, other people complain just the same way Mum did when you were at home. I think a lot of them go back to their parents and their parents can't believe the change in them: that they actually accept it as being fair now, instead of restriction.

Stuart: You can't really survive very well here unless you start, after a period of time, to think of other people; unless you take part in the community. You don't have cleaners rushing around after you, and over a period of time you develop a feeling for keeping a place reasonable and thinking of other people that you're living with. And that develops over the whole six-month programme. There's more beyond just talking about giving space to the individual; there is the practice of it. And it's so many different things — living in a block and being with other people, and being given the opportunity to sit and discuss what's happening to them all the time.

103

Mark: What sort of problems do hostel advisers have to deal with?

Rachel: A lot of the youngsters have problems concerning living in a community and finding out more about themselves — emotional problems, sometimes sexual problems, problems about sharing a room, domestic problems with cleanliness — that kind of thing. Hassles over the other person not making their bed and: "I don't want my friends to come and see a bed unmade." From very petty things to something much much bigger. There's a vast range of problems really.

Mark: On average how many people have you got to look after in the block?

Rachel: Well, there's myself and Janie in the block, looking after twenty-three.

Mark: That strikes me as an awful lot of people to have to look after in a pastoral way.

Stuart: One thing we try to do is to put the responsibility onto them to help each other. If you get into the situation where people only begin to survive by going to the staff with their particular problems, that's not achieving a tremendous amount because there's going to come a time when there are not people there to listen to them. So a lot of the time we try to say to them: "Look, things are going to come up, why don't you help each other, support each other, talk to each other", and we try to set up situations where they do this.

Mark: What would you say the main benefits are for people going out on a placement: what are they getting out of it?

Stuart: I would say that it is central to the whole Postern Programme. The work is like the skeleton of the Postern Programme: it's what initiates the self-discipline side from the beginning, because they have to make decisions, which have to do with getting to work on time and putting something into the work. If anyone actually leaves the Postern because they're not doing anything at work, it's their decision not anybody else's. By the time we've talked it through with them and given them the opportunity, it's their decision. But the other thing, I think, is just getting out, being with different people, being able to look objectively

104

again outside the place, and then coming back and sharing those experiences.

Mark: Do you reckon, on the whole, that you are successful?

Stuart: I'd say it's as important as Summerhill was. It's as important as any of those places. What we've been trying to do over the last three years, nobody has tried to do before. People have been scared of the kind of responsibility which is given to the people who come here, and the progress is phenomenal. I've never seen a place where people develop so much in such a short period of time.

Mark: What about the relationship between the Postern and the rest of Dartington?

Stuart: I think it is really a question of what Dartington thinks it's about and should be about. It's about people living together and trying to share things and show concern for each other — going through times when that doesn't happen and learning from that. It's about going out and meeting other people; it's about taking responsibilities within the community whenever possible; it's about looking at yourself in perspective and in relation to the outer world; and about where you're going, on a personal level. On those levels, I think it's very much like Dartington.

Mark: Rachel, what would you say you had gained from being a hostel adviser here?

Rachel: I always find it difficult to answer that question, because it's something that you can only fully realise after you've left. I know that I've got a lot out of it: I know I've developed, I've changed. One thing is just confidence in dealing with young people ... I can walk into a room and I don't feel tense or nervous: if I've got something to say I'll say it. I can handle that situation — it definitely is a two-way process. Also working with a staff group is something I'd never done before and it's as if we have our own tutor group here. We go into things with each other and try to be sensitive and aware of each other as well.

Stuart: That's very important, in the sense that we're going through the same process as the Posterners are — the learning. We have our own separate learning, and that's not an afterthought. I think we've always known that. That's what it is about, and that's just as important as what the Posterners get from it. Some of the house staff have really used the place to sort themselves out and to think about what they are going to do and then move on to other things.

Rachel: And really the anxieties the Posterners have are exactly the same as the anxieties that we have in terms of personality, relationships, or what the hell we're going to do when we leave the Postern. I know that I'm leaving in April and I've got exactly the same dilemma as the Posterners have as regards accommodation, work ... so that's all shared really. The age is irrelevant — we share the same kind of universal anxieties.

Stuart: Yes and that's really good because they see you — they do it after a very short while — just see you as human beings, with ups and downs and faults, the same as themselves. That's encouraging for them, instead of like a teacher constantly telling them what to do and giving them the impression that you know everything.

Sue: But part of it is that we can't hide our emotions from them really, so if you want to cry and they happen to be there, then you've got to cry and they're there and they're watching you; or if you get angry and they're there watching you. So it's all the same, you're just a part of the community really.

QUESTIONNAIRES WERE GIVEN to all the Posterners. Of these, 109 were returned, which represented 31% of those sent out. Their results can be summarised as follows:

1. Given a rating scale 1–5 for enjoyment of postern experience:

> 65% gave the highest rating
> 26% gave the second highest

2. Concerning employment, of those who have left the Postern:

> 32% have had some experience of employment but are not currently working
> 36% are currently working
> 12% are in full-time education
> 9% are taking an MSC or Government-sponsored course
> 11% have not had a job or course since leaving the Postern

106

3. Voluntary Work:

 22% of those who have left the Postern have become involved in voluntary work

4. New Activities:

 34% of those who have left the Postern claim to have become involved in new activities as a result of joining the Postern Programme

5. Important Elements of the Postern Programme:

In general, relationships were reported as the most important element in the Postern experience:

 65% regarded staff friendship as very important
 62% regarded friendships with each other as very important
 63% regarded community life as very important
 55% regarded staff advice as very important
 50% regarded the work done as very important
 46% regarded the course weeks as very important

Other aspects of the course mentioned on the questionnaire and shown to be significantly less important to ex-Posterners included:

 The opportunity to do exams
 Friday afternoon discussions
 Evening activities
 Support after leaving

A few examples of comments made by ex-Posterners in response to the questionnaire:

The Postern provided for me a sort of start to working life; it gave me a job, new friends and gave me confidence to try new things. It was the best thing I've ever done in my life to date.

The time I spent at the Postern was the most rewarding time of my life. I became more mature and more independent and able to cope with life.

I built a tremendous amount of confidence in communicating with people, and have found a 'lifetime' career to interest me (Postern introduced this to me). Many thanks.

The Postern Programme gave me inner confidence in myself and respect for other people, which in turn made it much easier to get the job that I wanted and enjoy so much.

I have gained a lot from the experience of the Postern, and without it would be a very different person.

There was always plenty to do and an excellent choice in both work and leisure activities.

How the hell can you let them close the programme down? I had the best time in my life there. Something, hopefully, I'll remember for the rest of my life. This kind of work community should be all over the country to show kids that there's more things to live for than 'mugging old ladies and causing vandalism'.

The Pottery Training Workshop: students with Peter Starkey (centre) and Peter Cook (far right), his assistant.

CHAPTER FIVE

The Pottery Training Workshop

T HE POTTERY TRAINING WORKSHOP did not represent a *direct* manifestation of the growing desire to rediscover the Estate in the 1970s, for the impulse to create the project came from outside Dartington. It was, nevertheless, ideally suited to the spirit that prevailed at the time it was proposed to the Trust. The crafts had, from the 1920s, played an important role at Dartington — though perhaps not quite as centrally as is often supposed. Craft work, as an alternative to industrial mass production, was an essential element within the tradition from which the Dartington experiment had grown. The relationship of the maker to his or her work, the quality of design and materials and the value of manual labour were all essential ingredients in the reconstruction of a 'full life' and integrated rural community. Pottery, which uses a raw material drawn directly from the earth, clay, was historically the 'first' of the crafts, and offered a fitting basis for the renaissance of craft activities at Dartington.

Besides, in the 1930s Bernard Leach had come to the Estate to run a pottery, the Elmhirsts had sponsored him on a visit to Japan, and it was at Dartington that he had written *A Potter's Book*. While Leach was in Japan, the Elmhirsts sponsored his son David for training in larger-scale pottery production at Stoke-on-Trent. They hoped that a Leach production workshop might be established at Dartington as another small rural industry offering employment and skills to the neighbourhood. This project never came to fruition, and the Leach's moved to

111

St. Ives. Leach's name continued to be associated with Darting-ton, however. It was not until the mid-1970s that the original idea of a Dartington workshop was to be revived, perhaps fittingly with the collaboration of David Leach.

It had become clear to many in the British pottery world by the early 70s, that existing provisions for training were highly inadequate. Art schools offered courses in ceramics and pottery, but they were neither specific nor practical enough: the institutions offering them were cut off from the commercial pressures of the world, and on graduating, students were still very much in need of 'real' training. There were only a very limited number of working potters to whom these graduates could apprentice themselves. Many graduates were forced to give up the idea of practising their craft, while a diminishing number of others turned to teaching, but as something of an expedient rather than a vocation.

During the early 1970s, David Canter, Secretary of the Craftsmen Potters' Association and the man behind the highly successful Cranks vegetarian restaurants, began working with David Leach on the idea of creating a training establishment outside the already existing formal institutions. David Canter became involved with the Dartington Hall Trust's plans to set up a commercial and educational centre at Shinners Bridge, on the edge of the Estate by the Totnes-Plymouth road. The idea of a training workshop seemed to fit ideally into the conception of a 'visitor centre' that was intended to be more than just a business. When David Canter was appointed a Project Director for what was to become the Dartington Cider Press Centre, his brief included the creation of the pottery training workshop.

From Dartington's point of view, the idea of the Cider Press Centre had arisen out of the need to develop and make use of a key but peripheral site on the Estate. Previously, the old farm buildings at Shinners Bridge had been used as a community centre; there had also been a shop, a restaurant, and Marianne de Trey's pottery, which used the workshop originally built for Bernard Leach. John Lane, one of the Trustees, developed a scheme which was loosely based on multiple-use conversions in the United States (the former Ghirardelli chocolate factory on the San Francisco waterfront, in particular), and entailed the development of a centre which would combine retail and exhibition areas, craft workshops and galleries. The centre would bring together Dartington's broad-ranging interests, and act as a kind of living embodiment of the Elmhirsts' ideas, through which visitors could learn about the Trust's work and history.

Ideally, the Cider Press Centre was to act as a kind of gateway in and out of Dartington — a means of approach for the visitor, as well as a way for the Estate to 'reach outwards'. The place of the crafts within such a conception was crucial, as they were seen to represent an essential complement (or, for some, an alternative) to Dartington's textile, furniture and glass factories. It was partly with this in mind that Maurice Ash, then Chairman of the Trust, presented the Cider Press as a new centre which would hopefully act as a point of focus for the whole community — Estate and parish — offering, among other things, a market for local produce and a meeting place for older people. Once again, Dartington's original vision had captivated the Trust, and the Pottery Workshop, with its bold combination of learning and earning seemed to provide a concrete first-step towards the development of a 'craft village' on the Estate — a faint but nevertheless genuine echo of the Tagore-inspired dreams that had launched the Dartington experiment.

The Dartington workshop was to be a pilot project that could be applied to other crafts at Dartington and duplicated in other parts of the country. The Cider Press Centre which, as well as regular exhibitions, would include a prestigious craft gallery selling the best of British work, would provide a unique opportunity for the workshop to retail its wares. This must have seemed almost too good to be true.

The Training Workshop was set up in 1975, with David Canter as Managing Director and a Board which included a number of leading practising potters such as David Leach, Mick Casson, Marianne de Trey and Colin Kellam, as well as representatives from the government's Crafts Advisory Committee (later known as the Crafts Council) and the Dartington Hall Trust, both of whom were sponsoring the project. As the original prospectus stated, the workshop had "been established for the

113

purpose of providing a period of practical training in actual workshop conditions, for students and apprentices intending to make a living by setting up their own workshop, or working for existing pottery workshops."

The pottery was intended to be a viable 'real world' business, with the trainees expected to work under the same disciplines as ordinary employees. The period of training might last one or two years, and was to provide "a thorough working knowledge of all the factors relating to the running of a production pottery, from the purchasing of raw materials, through the preparation of the clay bodies and the glazes, to the throwing and turning of the range of ware to a high standard of quality and accuracy of repetition." The trainees were also to be familiar, as far as was possible, with the mechanics of running a business and, perhaps over-optimistically, there was to be a 'co-partnership' scheme whereby the trainees received a share of any profits made by the workshop.

The Crafts Advisory Committee made a capital grant towards the conversion of the building, as well as giving a maintenance grant for the trainees. In return for these favour-able terms, which would make it possible for the workshop to trade without having to pay wages, the Committee stipulated that trainees should have a day a week to themselves, to pursue their own work.

The Board appointed Peter Starkey (who had trained at Har-row School of Art and set up his own pottery in Norfolk) as the Workshop's Manager. Starkey was highly regarded as a salt-glaze potter, but he had little managerial business experience. He was to be assisted by Peter Cook, who had also trained at Harrow. The pottery was to produce a range of high quality domestic stoneware with brush decoration, which Peter Starkey designed to a general brief from the Board. The first six trainees arrived in September 1976, only a few months after the first prototype had been approved. The number of trainees varied from six to eight, with a system of staggered admissions to the course to ensure a mix of 'green' and more experienced potters.

Between 1976 and 1981, eleven students between the ages of 18 and 45 graduated from Dartington. All of them went on to work as potters and six of them started their own workshops. The working conditions at the workshop were by no means ideal; managers and trainees had to work very long hours — particularly if they wished to give time to their own work — and the business was plagued from the start by financial worries.

Generally speaking, the training element in the workshop proceeded according to plan, with the students moving in stages from the most basic to the more sophisticated techniques involved, and getting a chance to try their hands at every aspect of the work, including book-keeping and marketing. There were intermittent programmes of talks given by potters, as well as the occasional session about running a small business or accounting.

By 1979, Peter Starkey had taken a job elsewhere and David Canter resigned as Managing Director. There were still far more applicants than the workshop could take on as trainees, and the pottery was finding a market. However, month by month the business's overdraft had been growing. Much to the Crafts Council's alarm, the '5th day', in which students could pursue their own work, had largely been abandoned in order to keep the commercial side of the business afloat. After Peter Starkey and David Canter's resignations, the role of Managing Director was taken over by an executive committee, chaired at first by David Leach and later by Marianne de Trey, and Peter Cook became the workshop's manager.

It was recognised that David Canter, whose extraordinary dynamism had helped get the workshop off the ground in the first place, had been over-stretched by his many and varied interests. There had been insufficient board meetings, and Peter Starkey, who was a much better teacher and potter than businessman, had been left carrying far too much in the way of responsibilities. The new executive committee, which included some of Dartington's financial and commercial staff under the chairmanship of a locally-based professional potter, would hopefully function more responsively and efficiently.

The workshop struggled on until 1984, when negotiations were begun for the sale of the business to its managers. While it is generally agreed that the pottery continued to offer a unique training opportunity, commercial viability remained an unachievable ambition, and the general atmosphere at the workshop was characterised by persistent anxiety. The mood was not improved when, in 1982/83, the operation was moved from the Cider Press Centre to a set of buildings a quarter of a mile away. The Dartington Hall Trust and Dartington Trading offered some compensation for the resulting shortfall in production, but the students felt resentful about having to spend time converting the new accommodation rather than making pottery.

John Lane, one of the Dartington Hall Trustees, took over as Chairman in December 1982. The tighter relationship with the Trust, while not being an easy one, probably helped force some of the workshop's inherent difficulties into the open. In 1983, the potter Janice Tchalenko — whose popular colourful work reflected a shift of fashion away from more traditional British ware — was invited to design a new range of Dartington pottery. This range proved to be enormously popular, and there is no doubt that the sudden promise of commercial success helped energise the pottery at this stage. The Crafts Council, however, had lost faith in the project and was no longer willing to guarantee support for trainees. It made sense at this point for Peter Cook (Manager), Stephen Course (Assistant Manager) and a new partner, Peter Hazell, to take on full financial responsibility for the workshop.

The new independent pottery was not set up as a 'training workshop': its first priority has clearly been financial viability, with any educational ambitions conditional upon economic strength — the number of trainees depending on the business's financial health. There are those who doubted that the success of a fashionable range would guarantee the workshop's longer-term viability in a rapidly shifting market. However, in the light of the many problems encountered by the Pottery Training Workshop during its first two years, there was reason to believe that the independent pottery's new sense of self-reliance might breed the kind of energy that would ensure a sound basis for continuity, as well as for a commitment to practical training.

WHY WAS THE Pottery Training Workshop not a success? Along with many other Dartington projects, the Pottery Training Workshop undoubtedly suffered from being overly dependent on the powers that had facilitated its creation. It had always been intended that the workshop should become (with continuing training grant support) financially independent. However, the nature of the project's initial and subsequent relationship to the Trust and to the Crafts Advisory Committee probably hindered the development of a sense of entrepreneurial self-reliance. The involvement of the Trust and Crafts Council in the project was double-edged: they made the workshop possible in the first place, but, in generously 'parenting' the venture, inevitably discouraged the fast growth of independence and energy that was needed. Furthermore, the locus of responsibility for the workshop was spread too widely, between various interest-groups and people with varying degrees of commitment to the venture.

The workshop was, in effect, set up in a kind of vacuum, only partially related to the demands and pressures of the real world. And although it was established under what seemed to be very favourable financial conditions, with capitalisation and maintenance grants from the Crafts Advisory Committee and support from the Trust — all of which should have given the business a head start — it could be argued that by beginning to train before firmly establishing the business, the project's creators were placing impossible demands on those who were running it.

When Alan Caiger-Smith, a highly experienced potter who has taken on a limited number of apprentices for many years, visited the Dartington workshop in 1979, he suggested that too much weight had been placed on the workshop's 'training' function: "It could be better thought of", he wrote, "as a practising workshop, trading and paying its way, which is also devised so that trainees will be a regular part of the workforce. Thus the trainees are first and foremost assistants in a business rather than students. I think they will actually get more benefit from this approach than from the apparently more lofty conception of the workshop as an educational centre."

117

Caiger-Smith suggested the abolition of the '5th day', and a disciplined working day with a 5 p.m. finish to work, rather than the much looser arrangement at Dartington in which personal and Dartington Pottery work inevitably competed. Caiger-Smith also recommended that the Manager should "depend on the business for a significant part of his income", rather than rest secure in the knowledge of a regular salary.

In setting up a workshop which placed equal value on commercial viability and education, the founders of the Dartington Pottery were inevitably faced with the problem of finding a Manager who could fulfill an almost impossible range of functions — including teaching, business, design, production and managerial abilities. "The snag lies", as one adviser to the pottery pointed out after the resignation of the first manager, Peter Starkey, "in the fact that anyone who can run the Training Workshop properly is also likely to be able to run his own business equally well, and might well prefer to do the latter, enjoying the freedom as well as the risk it entails, rather than opt for the Training Workshop." Workshop managers have in fact always been much stronger on production and teaching than on business and management, and this is reflected in the enthusiastic reactions from past trainees, most of whom place great value on the 'educational' side of their experience at Dartington.

The Dartington Pottery Training Workshop's failure to achieve commercial viability is related as well to the problems that inevitably arise out of Dartington's creative patronage: the resources that make experiment possible and enable the Trust to set up projects which break down the barriers between 'learning' and 'earning', also have an inevitable tendency to insulate projects rather too well from the commercial demands of the real world. In the Pottery Training Workshop's case, the instigators of the project were only partly involved — David Canter was equally absorbed in many other projects, whilst David Leach and others were busy running their own potteries. The Trust and the Crafts Council, as the sources of finance, were naturally distanced from the Workshop's day-to-day existence. As one ex-trainee wrote in 1985, she had felt that the

118

most important decisions were being taken by 'outsiders', however benevolently disposed.

The ambivalence and failure to engage, which is reflected in Dartington's relationship to the Cider Press and Pottery Training Workshop, arises in part from the consequences of the Elmhirsts' own early withdrawal from direct participation, and their establishment of a 'Trust' which by its very nature implied a rather detached form of guardianship rather than intensive commitment.

The Cider Press, which was in 1976 seen as providing a focus for renewed activity in the village of Dartington, has never in fact fulfilled the promise of a commercially-viable setting for learning by doing which at the same time serves as a community centre to the village. This was in part because David Canter, who directed the project with considerable independence, was an outsider and therefore had a rather limited feel for the place in which he was working, but this goal is anyway not a very realistic one in the circumstances. It was not surprising that the Cider Press Centre should feel like something of a graft onto the Estate. Local reactions both at the time and since, have reflected a feeling that no matter how successful, the Centre does not exactly feel a part of the 'village'.

While the original plan had placed a great emphasis on the educational side of the Cider Press, commercial imperatives have grown increasingly central. The Pottery Training Workshop, which originally carried, more than any other part of the Cider Press, the hope that old categories might be overcome and goals fundamentally re-aligned, found itself uneasily caught in the Cider Press's shift towards increasingly commercial goals. It cannot have been a comfortable place to be, although the Centre did provide an easily accessible retail outlet. Instead of proving to be the first of a number of craft workshops on the site — a nucleus for the renewal of community — the Pottery became increasingly isolated, the only 'educational' venture left in a complex of commercial enterprises that catered primarily to the tourist trade.

In 1982, the Pottery was moved in order to release the premises it was occupying for more cost-effective use. The divorce between Dartington's purely commercial drive and its more fluid and experimental ventures into 'earning and learning' was being re-enacted, the Trust once again in ambivalent retreat from its original intentions. The Pottery survived to become, in 1985, independent from its original sponsors. The present owners hope to continue offering a context in which potters can gain experience, but the training will not be formalised, and those who come to the pottery to learn will be, as Alan Caiger-Smith suggested, 'assistants in the business' rather than students. At the time of writing, the range of pottery designed by Janice Tchalenko is selling very well, but only time will tell whether the pottery can flourish both as a business and as a place of practical learning.

POTTERY TRAINING AT DARTINGTON
— SOME EX-TRAINEES LOOK BACK

*I*N 1984, before the Trust and Crafts Council withdrew their support, a number of ex-trainees from the Pottery Training Workshop were asked to reflect on their two years at Dartington: what
they had got out of it, and what they considered to be the most
positive and negative aspects of the training.

The Workshop taught me many things. Probably the most useful was
repetition throwing — I was six months on four sizes of jugs. I found it
pretty hard-going to just be making jugs all the time but it is the sort of
experience that is very useful afterwards. In a way, the workshop
experience was masochistic; where else are you into work by 7.30
a.m./8.00 a.m., until anytime in the evening, freezing cold, doing the
same thing at weekends for yourself, and basically physically very
uncomfortable for £16 per week. But it gave me commercial
experience I wouldn't otherwise have had and also an opportunity to
work with Peter Starkey, whom I regarded as Britain's No. 1 Salt Glaze
Potter, and was the main reason I wanted to go there.

The workshop's problems when I was there were all teething
problems. I was the fifth person to join the workshop and only the
basics had been sorted out. We had the space and Pete Cook
and Pete Starkey had built the kiln. But the logistics of how it was
all going to work still had to be sorted out, plus the range of pots
to be made, type of decoration etc.

I definitely think the combination of working business and training is useful.

I FIND IT DIFFICULT to think clearly about Dartington. Whilst now
being very glad for the experience gained (and certainly my time
here [West Surrey College of Art & Design] has been far richer
due to that past experience) I did not at the time have enough
previous experience to really make full use of the opportunity. I
can only feel that two years at the Dartington Pottery Training
Workshop would be far more pertinent after college, where it
certainly has a very valuable and important role. However it can
in no way be a substitute for three years on a BA ceramics
course. Dartington Pottery Training Workshop or any production
workshop is dealing with very different issues and the area where
the two overlap is really quite small.

121

'What did the Workshop teach me?' Throwing experience was very valuable as was the day-to-day running of a workshop; how to mix clay, glazes, pack and fire a kiln etc. And these skills are certainly more efficiently learnt in a workshop situation than in college.

I must confess that the economics of the Dartington Pottery Training Workshop were always somewhat baffling. We were earning a very low wage (a grant, in fact) and yet not as I remember making a profit at that time. But I guess I did gain some sense of how firings must run according to schedule and other useful things.

The Workshop was having financial problems. The nature of these problems wasn't quite clear and therefore it was difficult to really develop awareness of business sense. And maybe the Workshop's lack of autonomy did not help foster this awareness. Despite trainees attending business meetings it did often seem that the economic issues were in other people's hands (i.e. the Trust?) and therefore it was more difficult to actually get to grips with that side of things than if one was in a workshop without those kind of links and complex involvements, however necessary and helpful they were.

The 5th-day concept was excellent. It only happened a few times when I was there, due to the financial problems, but I think it now operates successfully.

WHAT THE WORKSHOP taught me was basically what I needed to learn. Its problems in my opinion were: a) it tried aiming at a too high class market — for a workshop with such a fast turnover of students, it made everything a bit up-tight; b) there seemed a real confusion over its image, educational, commercial, educational-commercial or commercial-educational?

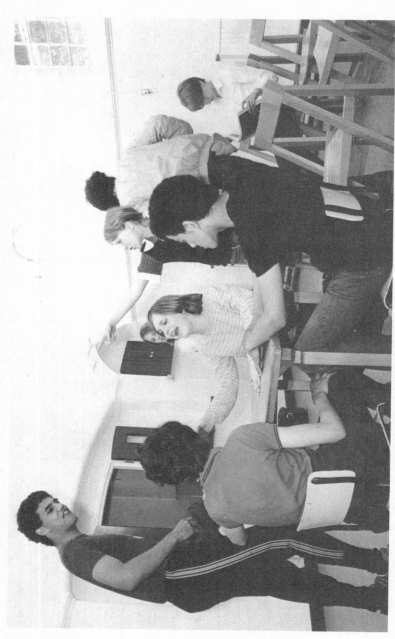

Dartington College of Arts Theatre Department's base at Rotherhithe in London; student working with teenagers (*photo Graham Green*).

CHAPTER SIX

Taking the Arts out of the College

THE THIRD YEAR of Dartington's four-year theatre course is spent almost entirely outside the recognised boundaries of the College: each student spends the year 'making theatre' in Rotherhithe, Devon, or further afield, away from the lecture room, studio or library. The other courses at the College reflect, although to a lesser extent, a similar bias towards learning from direct experience, beyond the shelter of the institution. Not only does the College extend informally into the world, with the students learning by doing, but the notion of 'art' itself is being redefined and broadened, through a training that is designed to prepare the students for a role as enablers and community workers, instead of just developing their own talents as professional artists.

The arts, as understood by the College, reach out beyond the cocoon-like privilege of galleries, concert-halls and West End theatres. The artist should, ideally, be fully engaged with the world around him, taking his or her particular talents or vision into the streets, schools, hospitals or prisons. Rather than approach art objects or performances as consumers, ordinary people who might not regard themselves as artists should be able to take part in creative processes — whether individually or as part of a group. Access to the arts suggests, according to this view, active involvement rather than a more passive role as audience. Such participation allows for a 'doing' that opens up opportunities for learning, both in terms of personal discovery, and also exploration and creative

125

intervention in the world. In a specialised society, the artist monopolises a role which might, in a more integrated context, be shared more widely.

The College's wish to make the arts more accessible has been strengthened by a general cultural trend that has grown since the 1960s, with the rise of the community arts movement; it also reflects a longer-term connection with Dartington's own tradition. The arts have always played a central role in the myth that sustains Dartington. The 'full life' envisaged by the Elmhirsts encompassed the arts, as well as education, business, farming, forestry and all the other activities which were to help revitalise the Estate and its surroundings. Theatre, dance, printing, sculpture and music, however, were not just seen as recreational extra-curricular attractions, or a cultural bonus for the workers: they were to provide a much-needed channel for personal expression and contact with inner life, as well as a catalyst for community. As Dorothy Elmhirst explained: "It was never intended to make Dartington an economic experiment, merely concentrating on farming, forestry and rural industry. From the beginning, we envisaged something more — a place where education could be continuously carried on and where the arts could become an integral part of the life of the whole place. We believed that not only should we provide for the mutual well-being of people here but for the cultural and social needs as well."

Leonard and Dorothy Elmhirst believed that direct and practical involvement in the arts allowed for the rediscovery of territory which much institutionalised religion had turned into a waste land. Such an approach had been essential to Rabindranath Tagore's vision of a re-constituted village community, with the practice of the arts and crafts woven into the fabric of everyday life.

From the early days, the Elmhirsts invited artists to Dartington with a view to sharing their talents with as many people on the Estate and beyond as possible. There were community plays and dance-mime productions directed by Margaret Barr, and painting classes with Mark Tobey and Cecil Collins. The arrival of the Kurt Jooss Ballet and the establishment of the Chekhov Theatre Studio in the mid-1930s, however, created a major rift

126

between professional and amateur artists. Both organisations worked within a 'professional' framework. The artists at Dartington became a caste apart — Bohemian outsiders with no more than a fleeting investment in Estate life.

However much the Elmhirsts were drawn into playing the part of patrons of the avant-garde during the Thirties, they did remain in part faithful to the idea of making the arts widely available, as Dartington's later history clearly demonstrates. Imogen Holst, who ran courses for music teachers at Dartington in the 1940s, encouraged everyone on the Estate to learn a musical instrument: even Leonard Elmhirst took up the cello in his sixties. The development of the Arts Centre into the College of Arts, the work of Peter Cox, showed a continuing concern on the part of the Elmhirsts for wider participation in the arts — in the early College's case through the training of teachers.

In the 1960s, when Dartington expanded its activities to North Devon, the establishment of a glassworks at Torrington was accompanied by the creation of the Beaford Arts Centre, which was described as a pioneering venture in 'rural animation'. Beaford, as well as offering residential courses, promoted exhibitions, concerts and performances in the more remote towns and villages. By sponsoring events in pubs and village halls, the Centre did make a serious attempt at extricating such events from isolation and prejudice. Dartington's commitment to the idea of making the arts central to life was still strong.

The College's existing courses express the same concern, but basic contradictions remain; for the gap between the arts as practised today and the needs of ordinary people is, on the whole, very wide. The artist in a fragmented society tends to reflect the many dualisms and oppositions which tear the body social apart: the artist is, almost inevitably, driven to question, criticize and undermine a state of affairs that is, in terms of feeling or spiritual values, intolerable. The artist as outsider, however, fits uneasily into the conformism of a mass society, in which individuals feel disturbed or threatened by alternatives to consensus reality.

The task of reintegrating the arts, as in the case of education, requires a fundamental change in world-view as much as social structure — a change that has, at present, little more substance than a dream. It is this powerful image, however, which may underlie the College's interest in 'art and design in social contexts' and 'theatre in the community', although the deeper and more radical concerns are often somewhat obscured by an attitude which focuses exclusively on the problem of elitism in the arts. This issue is crucial, yet its scope falls far short of Tagore's understanding of what reintegration might mean.

The reintegration of the arts into the mainstream of life demands a particular kind of training. The fine art or dance studio, the 'life' and movement class, or the writing workshop, will help develop a student's skill, but there is also clearly a particular need for 'learning by doing' — for as much interaction as possible with a given community. The themes that underlie Dartington's approach to education in the arts require, almost by definition, a commitment to a large measure of training outside institutional boundaries.

All three courses at Dartington — theatre, art and music — attempt in their different ways to place their students in the everyday world outside the College. In the music department's case this remains an option, Music in Society, which takes students to Bristol for most of a term; others go into local schools, and a number work with handicapped children and adults. In the art department, all students choose a 'placement' during their second year, and all the theatre students spend a third year 'out', in Rotherhithe, Devon or further afield. [The term 'placement' is no longer (Jan 89) used by the College, as it has been appropriated by industry to cover paid work. The art department is now concerned with various 'models of interactive arts work', an idea which each student will interpret in a slightly different way. I have, however, for the sake of brevity and clarity used the former term throughout.]

Dartington's art and design course is one of the few in the country that offer a training for students who wish to work in the community. Other courses use placements, but only a small number of colleges share Dartington's policy commitment to "a more convincing public role for the arts". The idea of the course is, according to those who run it, "to offer a practical art

education to students who expect eventually to work in art
with people in local settings, (as opposed to work geared to the
gallery world)." The course emphasises "group work, the placing of images in everyday settings, the study of images
commonly available through TV, newspapers etc."

The students are encouraged, above all, to explore "ways of
producing art in response to particular settings or groups of
people". The emphasis, therefore, is not so much on facilitating
participation, as it is on an immersion in the world outside the
studio, with a view to stimulating student response, in his or
her capacity as aspiring artist.

During the early part of the course, students are introduced
to "approaches and skills relevant to socially oriented work".
Later, they are gradually eased into various community projects
which might include public sculpture, murals, design for performance, or tape-slide work. Before completing their degree,
all are required to choose settings outside the College to which
their work will relate. The placements have varied widely and
have included prisons, hospitals, community centres, schools
for the handicapped, a slimming club, the local zoo, and many
others.

The placements are not 'work experience' in the accepted
sense, for each student is expected to respond individually to a
chosen setting: the student very much creates his or her own
work rather than adapting to an already existing set of relationships and expectations, or serving the needs of those on the
receiving end of the placement. The placements are "essentially
projects done with reference to a location or a group ... the idea
is to choose a setting where art is not normally practised and to
find within it a role for art."

The ideal placement stimulates personal engagement and
creativity in the student and produces work which in some way
opens up communication with an 'audience' that would normally not look at art. In one case, a student interested in the
effects of medical technology on childbirth chose two comparative placements, a natural childbirth group and an NHS ante-
natal clinic. Both welcomed her and provided opportunities for
drawing and research. On the basis of this work, the student

made an 'installation' that presented, with great passion, her reactions to the effects on women of machinery and mechanistic ways of thinking. After the work had been finished, she invited groups of women to view the piece. In this particularly success-ful case, the placement had provided both a source and a public for the student's work.

Not all placements have been as successful, for schools and community centres, for example, expect the students to offer something more than 'art' in return for their openness and hospitality. The students can find themselves being edged into the role of 'animateurs', teachers or community workers. Naturally, the expectations arising from the particular settings often have little to do with the artistic concerns of the students, who come in more senses than one as outsiders.

The placements do not just demand an exploratory attitude from the students. The same is expected from the communi-ties they join. The students and their potential public or 'community' are involved in a radical experiment: the rediscovery of art forms which derive their meaning from collective rather than personal concerns and perspectives. The burden on relatively young and inexperienced students is, naturally, very great, and they are not always able to find a middle ground in which personal motivation and collective concerns can meet.

Part of the art course's problem arises, no doubt, from the conflict between the individual needs of students who, in-fluenced by a fine art culture which has evolved in a highly individualistic way since the Renaissance, are trapped bet-ween an image of themselves as individual artists, with all the cultural and personal expectations that this self-definition brings, and the radical aims of a course which envisages the development of public rather than private art forms. The rediscovery of a common language, within the context of a secularised and fragmented culture which depends so heavily on television, is by no means an easy journey, and many of the students have found themselves drawn into taking up ideologically derived positions, which confront rather than transcend, and divide, rather than integrate.

Such a response may be inevitable for young artists who have chosen to question the practices of the gallery world and art market, but there is a danger that an embattled reaction to such values can lead to a rather sterile and oppositional stance, which is trapped in a primarily materialistic world-view, and out of touch with concerns and images that might help re-establish a deep and lasting connection between the arts and the average person in the street.

This danger is greater for the art students who are, to a large extent, tied to the production of art objects, than it is for those who take the four-year theatre course. Theatre is a more accessible form than visual art; non-professionals can be involved with much greater ease in the process of 'making theatre'. Theatre has roots in communal ritual and archaic images; there is also a very long-standing tradition of theatre as popular entertainment. It provides, for these reasons, ideal ground for bringing people together, and rediscovering a common language. At Dartington it has been the theatre course, not surprisingly, which has made the most important recent contribution to the practice of community arts. The course has also gone furthest in relating the students' learning process to experience in the world, for the 'year out', un-like the placements on the art course, involves immersion in an already established community-based project. Whereas, on the art course, each student creates her or his own placement, the theatre students can often slot into a pre-existing project which has established a network of relationships within the community. The student is expected to make an original contribution, but always being mindful of existing expectations and the need for con-tinuity.

DARTINGTON'S THEATRE COURSE trains 'theatre practitioners', and the course includes the development of writing, acting and directing skills, as well as opportunities to explore dance and community work. Much of the academic input to the course is intended to give students a sense of the theatre's origins in traditional cultures, as well as of the problems of contemporary communities. By the time the second year is over, students should be ready to take on the commitment of 'making theatre' outside the sheltered world of Dartington. Third year students can choose between a rural setting — the South Hams in Devon, close to Dartington, an urban project in London, and more recently a wider range of situations further afield.

The first base for the 'year out' was set up in 1975, as the Plymouth Action Community Theatre (PACT). It was originally based at the Arts Centre, but in 1978 moved to the Frederick Street Centre in Stonehouse — one of the city's most 'difficult' areas. The ground was laid by three former Dartington students and two members of staff. By the time the first group of third year degree students had arrived in 1977, PACT had its own premises in Stonehouse, in a former Tile Warehouse, which was converted with the help of local labour. PACT operated until the mid-1980s and was then closed down.

The London base was set up in 1978 in Rotherhithe. It was based in a warehouse by the edge of the Thames. The Rotherhithe Theatre Workshop has become one of the key cultural agencies in the area, and provides a means whereby each new year of Dartington students can become involved in the community. Between 1978 and 1985, seven successive groups of students worked in Rotherhithe, alongside staff from Dartington's theatre department. Between them, they made contact with a large number of local groups and organisations, including schools, youth groups, tenants' associations, day centres and pre-school groups.

The students' brief has always been: "to make theatre within a particular situation, and with and for particular people". The challenge which this presents for them cannot be under-estimated, particularly after two relatively secure years in rural Devon. The students who, on arrival, are likely to find themselves rather disorientated, are expected to organise their own learning process, to make relationships with a wide range of local people, and to 'make theatre'. Not only are they expected to maintain the context created by previous groups of students, but they also have to collaborate tactfully with others in the area, including social workers, tenants' associations, school authorities, architects and neighbours.

Describing the initial impact on students starting the 'year out', Graham Green, formerly in charge of the Plymouth venture, wrote that "local people may not want them, many question their motives, many come from a different social class or at least from a sub-culture that it would take (on the face of it) a lifetime or more, a 'history', to penetrate; most likely people will treat them and their work with a kind indifference. Some will need and welcome them: most usually the young, the elderly and the disadvantaged."

Working within the context of the College, students make theatre in a highly specialised and sympathetic environment. The year out, on the other hand, inevitably provokes them to question the value and nature of 'theatre', as well as their own motivations. The support supplied by the existing workshops and informal teaching, administration and community liaison staff is very limited, and each student has to find her or his own feet in a new and foreign environment. The theatre department's urban outposts have been depressed and depressing areas, in sharp contrast to Dartington's idyllic setting. The students have also had to learn to work as a group, and social ties that may have functioned on Dartington's secure home ground may be heavily strained by adverse conditions. Alongside these adjustments, the students have also to devise their own programme of work. This too offers an important but potentially very rewarding challenge, for each of them has to find a way of combining individual needs with those of the community. There must be a common ground, but never at the expense of the student's or the community's potential creativity.

"The scope for 'learning through doing', for each student" Graham Green wrote in a paper on the Plymouth Workshop, "is enormous; the situation is the great teacher, even if the lessons are often hard and confusing. As an educational possibility, the projects are effective and, for some students, the most memorable and affecting part of their work. Some students 'find' their work through this experience."

In Plymouth, students were involved in setting up major community events including large-scale events in the city's streets. They made weekly visits to hospitals, schools and senior citizen centres, as well as running a youth theatre, working with a women's group and unemployed teenagers.

In Rotherhithe, Dartington's project has played a key role in stimulating theatre-making in the community. As a member of Rotherhithe Theatre Workshop put it: "The theatre makers of Rotherhithe are the people who live in Rotherhithe. Together many now share a vision of a neighbourhood theatre programme devised, initiated and presented by themselves." By 1984, over 200 local people had become involved in theatre work. Student-initiated activities have included a weekly workshop for girls from two housing estates, a monthly evening meeting for the visually handicapped organised with the Social Services Department, and weekly contracts with local schools, youth clubs and an over-50's club.

Inevitably, the College's base in London has developed a strong identity of its own — more so than the Stonehouse workshop ever did, as the latter naturally maintained closer links with Dartington. The Rotherhithe Theatre Workshop undoubtedly has needed to feel strongly connected with the community in which it operates, for it is this sense of belonging which gives the venture strength and local credibility: when the students arrive from Dartington, they stand a much better chance of being accepted than if the workshop were simply a Dartington colony. The distance from Dartington is necessary, but it inevitably leads to a difference in perspectives and associated communication difficulties. The Rotherhithe Theatre Workshop experiences something of the same unavoidable isolation as did the School's Yorkshire and Sicily Projects in the early 1970s.

NOT SURPRISINGLY, the College's exploration of an education that moves outwards into the world, reveals the same paradoxical conflicts as have been evident in Dartington's other attempts at integrating 'learning' and 'doing', 'education' and 'work'. By virtue of Dartington's contemporary status as an institution with various 'departments', each of which has particular links with and pressures from other institutions, the Estate as a whole has become fragmented by institutional imperatives and specialisation.

The College has broken boundaries and sought to restore the arts to their proper place, but the immediate boundaries between College and Estate have remained almost completely unbroken, with the arts as distant as ever from the everyday lives of most Dartington employees. The 'community', for the College, begins beyond Dartington-owned land and businesses. While work in the cities and elsewhere beyond Estate boundaries is essential, it is sad that stronger connections at home cannot also be made, for the idea of community arts, however strongly it might take root in Rotherhithe, for instance, remains at Dartington itself an ideal rather than a reality.

Some of the College's staff are aware of the conflicting and uncomfortable currents that run through their work. They do not pretend to have found absolute solutions, and it is also clear that the students are involved in something far greater than their own personal exploration: they are also taking part in a difficult social and cultural experiment. Whatever ambiguities and difficulties may characterise the placements or year out, they do, in their different ways, reflect a courageous attempt at breaking new ground. Dartington's courses have to work within the framework of experiment; risking, as Leonard Elmhirst would have put it, 'positive or negative results'.

In Tagore's Bengali village, which so inspired Leonard Elmhirst, the vivification of the arts and the reconstruction of a culture which gave them a central place in everyday life was not, relatively speaking, such a difficult task: the patterns of traditional culture may have been in decline, but they were nevertheless strong enough to respond to re-animation. In the case of our own culture, the depth of dissociation between work, the arts and spiritual life is such that the way forward towards any degree of reintegration is not clear.

The Theatre course's year out probably offers students a fuller educational opportunity than the much less intense placement on the art course. In the latter case, the artist must, almost by definition, remain detached, contributing a refined vision of his/her key subject, even if this is derived from a social rather

135

than a personal context. The theatre student, however, has the chance to become immersed: can live and learn, for a year at least, within a particular working context. Such a commitment offers greater possibilities for learning. The year out offers, as did the Postern Programme, an all-round initiation, for it demands considerable commitment whilst at the same time provoking, through challenge, a greater opportunity for self discovery.

There is a note to be made here, of a proposal for an integrated arts course which did not progress beyond the exploratory committee stage. However, although it never came to anything, the idea is highly relevant to any discussion of Dartington's ambivalence towards the practical implications of putting its dreams into practice. Colette King, formerly head of the Theatre Department and the creator of the 'year out', suggested setting up a course of up to seven years length which would combine practical training in the arts with a series of apprenticeships to the varied crafts and trades on the Estate. The 'course' would be unequivocally rooted in the Dartington ground with a flow of ideas, skills and people between professionals and non-professionals. The course would train for 'living' as well as for 'making theatre', and might involve the students in growing some of their own food and directly looking after other material aspects of their lives.

The proposal was greeted with a mixture of apathy and derision: it was, for most, hopelessly idealistic and out-of-touch with the exigencies of a state-supported higher education. It was, however, totally in tune with Dartington's underlying concern for 'community', 'wholeness' and 'meaning', as well as being bold and imaginative. Such a scheme offered, in terms that may have at the time appeared unrealistic, the kind of framework upon which new inter-connecting patterns could have been laid. The proposal and the negative reactions to it demonstrated, at the very least, how much Dartington had become estranged from the adventure launched so bravely by the Elmhirsts, and nevertheless the proposal demonstrated that the image of an integrated Estate and a 'full life' has not been completely forgotten.

THE YEAR OUT — THE STUDENTS' EXPERIENCE

*A*FTER THE 'YEAR OUT' *each student on the four year Theatre BA course at Dartington College of Arts, has to write a long essay about his or her experiences. The following extracts, from a number of different students' work, were originally selected for publication in Dartington Voice in February 1983. We have kept the headings "Places", "People", "The Handicapped", "Teaching" and "An Event", originally used in the selection published by Dartington Voice.*

PLACES

PLYMOUTH, A CITY BROKEN, remoulded and hastily pieced back together again. Initially it left me cold. Even as a seven year old child I can remember visiting it with my parents and feeling exactly the same; who would ever have known I was due to pay that city another visit in fifteen years time. On a later visit at the age of fifteen, my sentiments were still the same; I picnicked out of a van full of hay with my cousins on the sidewalk just a little way up from 52 North Road, East. By then I was quite sure Plymouth was definitely not a place in which one would choose to live. Seven years later there I was, walking that very street, every day for nine months, only by then my sentiments had changed to — how on earth was anyone supposed to create in surrounds such as these. Boy, did my eyes need ungluing. Sources for material were so abundant and varied we were almost tripping over them but I couldn't see it. It's other human beings we should look towards more than material objects in the long run; isn't it?

ALONGSIDE ALL these struggles with work and principles, and half-formed ideas of what theatre is, there was another crucial factor affecting us all, and that was the influence of the environment. It is absolutely vital, when working within a community, that you live there too. Rotherhithe has a very particular environment — the bleak roads by the docks, the Dickensian wharves and ware-houses, piles of rubble and torn corrugated-iron fences down by the beach, the faceless housing blocks. There is a large park in the middle of it all, but the contrast of the open grass and trees is so great that it gives the quiet of the park a desperate edge, and

137

the inside is as dirty as out on the road. I took some lessons in photography at the Community Workshop and spent a day in January with Guy practising using the camera. On that day especially I became very aware of colours and the textures of the area: grey and brown, the harshness of brick and stone everywhere, and no horizon. We went into the park and saw an old man sitting on a bench. Guy stayed behind with the camera, and I went and sat beside him — we chatted about the unexpected sunshine, and he gave me a toffee. A few minutes later Guy came up — he was wearing his leather jacket, and smoking, and did not say a word; and suddenly the old man got up and hurried away. We realised afterwards that we must have frightened him; we felt dreadful and horrified at our lack of consideration — and at his keen sense of danger even at lunchtime in the park on a sunny day!

Tearing down posters at Surrey Docks with wording such as "Stop Malignant Aliens" may have been irresistible but could also have been foolish and dangerous. Southwark Park might not lie in the deepest pockets of hostility but it was there that Wole was threatened with a gun. In smaller ways most of the students felt threatened, at some point, in that environment. The reports of its being a 'rough' area seemed exaggerated in the first weeks. No violence directly confronted the newcomer; no open rejection shocked. But as the atmosphere of the place became part of life and the rhythm installed itself under the skin, the growing sense of isolation and not-belonging took its toll.

PEOPLE

PHILIP IS A TALL MAN thirty eight years old, whose communication is always a straight line out, then nothing, then another straight line. The undulations are completely missing. Such words as "and", "because", "why" are lacking in his vocabulary. A recital of his activities will have no continuity, it will be a block, pause, block. It is hard to get him to talk about himself, or his surroundings. And I must admit my total helplessness. I have never really managed to have contact with him.

KAY CAME as frequently as she could, but she was having difficulty with her weight, often feeling too insecure to come to sessions and then wanting to wear most of my clothing. One day Kay stopped coming altogether. It finally dawned on us why none of them had

138

seemed particularly bothered by us admitting that we could only work with them for nine months. Kay had been uprooted and moved to Exeter. She was the first. We had neither realised nor had anyone informed us that as Parklands was an assessment centre. Most kids did not stay more than a few weeks before being moved elsewhere (other residential homes, foster or adoptive parents, or Detention Centres). Kay wrote to me and said that she would still like to come to the drama sessions, but in the end it was agreed that it was too far to travel from Exeter to Plymouth, and she was not responsible and trustworthy enough to look after herself.

ONE GROUP OF BOYS, about seven 12 — 14 year-olds made their presence felt. A noteworthy member of the gang went by the name of Spud: a person of short stature and generous circumference with a five-millimetre fuzz adorning his pale scalp. These boys were lively contributors to the play and undoubtedly the perpetrators of the major thefts. They appeared at the door of the hall and wanted to know if their part in the play could take the form of dressing up as members of the Klu Klux Klan. It was suggested that they communicate this idea to Adewole. He discouraged this particular line of invention; they contented themselves with taking the parts of wizards and warlocks. Spud took great pains over spraying his 'bovver boots' silver for the occasion.

SHE TOLD ME: "I stood up one day and said, 'go screw yourself', and threw the teapot at him, and he said: 'what d'you mean; you never sew a pair of socks for me — Sew your own fucking socks!' and the needlework basket went at him. And then I joined Karate lessons, 'cos I'd got a few wallops before, and then he came for me once after that and I threw him across the front room, and I said: 'I know I'm a woman, but I'm equal to you now.' And he never came near me again."

THE HANDICAPPED

R. WAS THE MOST COHERENT of all the chaps. Sometimes we'd have long conversations during which he'd ask if certain cinemas or shops were still standing, and tell me about old Plymouth. He used the expression 'San Fairyann up Chapel Street', which means 'in a very bad way'. It was important to R. and J.W. that I was from Plymouth, where they used to live. It took ages for R. to say relatively little as, like the others who spoke, his speech had retrogressed over the years and was difficult to understand. He confided in me that he felt very guilty for having disgraced his mother "by being put in 'ere". I think the chaps were less willing to confide in me than the Martinsgate and Parklands kids were, because of the age difference.

R. was very changeable, and as often as he'd talk to me he'd tell me to "fuck off" and threaten me with violence which I once witnessed him using on a domestic.

One afternoon he seemed quite friendly and, investigating my bag, said "what've you brought in?" (I often took objects and postcards to show). He studied my cheque book with great interest, but quickly rejected a book of colour plates of Gainsborough's paintings, saying they didn't concern him. We started to read a Ted Hughes poem together when he snapped that he hated it and that I should wrap the book in brown paper. He then got on the floor saying "of course, I'm as mad as a hatter you know", and crawled away.

The next time I saw him he snarled an insult and retired to the bathroom.

A week later he approached and asked me to come to a corner, where he produced a crumpled piece of paper upon which he had written in illegible handwriting a poem entitled "Remembering". With obvious emotion he then sang the poem. It was about a girl he'd had a soft spot for when he'd been a young man in Plymouth. I told him it was beautiful and thanked him for singing it to me and he squeezed my hand, saying he'd never have thought of writing a poem if it hadn't been for me. He promised to copy it out into neater handwriting and give me a copy. He said it had been difficult to carry a pen because when he reached into his jacket for his pipe he'd grab the pen by mistake.

On my next visit, I couldn't see R. anywhere and asked where he was. He'd died three days after our meeting.

In Moorhaven, R. had on one occasion insulted me and threatened me with violence, yet on another occasion read me a poem and showed me gratitude. Where was the real R? Was he present in both incidents, one incident, or neither?

MICHAEL, who was one of the most loving and energetic kids in our group — who as yet had had the greatest difficulty in expressing himself within a group context (i.e. in the circle, where he felt pressure and fear at having to perform) — actually crossed his own boundary. We were asking simply that each should walk across the circle, approach another, say his/her name and change places with that person. Michael, till this specific afternoon had found this impossible. His usual reaction was to clam up, giggle and hide his face. I have no idea why this afternoon was different, but when his turn came he walked across the circle and said his name. I (and he) could not quite believe it. The joy in his face was extraordinary and after his break-through (for that is how I see it) he did not want to stop. I saw the courage he had summoned in order to perform that simple task and how, too, with the silent encouragement of the group, he had been able to express the simple fact that he was Michael.

A DEAF PERSON has no real concept of time. If you ask him to think back he has not got the facility to do it nor has he any real notion of time in the future. All he can report about is the immediate, what is happening to him at that moment in time. The subtlety of emotions are very important because they are potent to his physical awareness of what is going on around him. It is a very sensual world. However, the deaf have developed a much wider vocabulary to express innermost feelings than speech can facilitate. This is because words are not powerful enough to carry the real emotions and the true emotive force gets watered down or made unclear. It's very difficult to describe how we feel so we show it as best we can.

Therefore, because the deaf are used to expressing emotion in their faces and bodies, their expression is much more refined and subtle. This subtle interchange that happens in body communication is often difficult to use in performance because people are not used to perceiving it. It is a secondary mode of expression, so we pay little attention to it. It could easily be lost in performance. That is why most mime artists exaggerate gestures to make them more lucid. I find this a great shame.

TEACHING

WE SAT IN A CIRCLE on the floor. We started to play. For the first time during these sessions the room was still. The game imposed its own discipline. The level of concentration was unusually high. It was going smoothly until Paul obtained the dido. Paul was generally a very quiet, but stubbornly uncooperative character whom I suspected of having a vicious streak. As soon as the dido was in his hands, two of the other young men disobeyed by lying down. They refused to take notice of any of his orders. I, most respectfully, made a suggestion to Paul — note the stupidity of the 'teacher's' suggestion — that he could organise us into two groups who could then physically force Ian and Peter to sit up.

He had barely nodded when everyone pounced on the two unfortunate lads. What I had not heard, was that Paul had said "Yeah, and duff 'em over while you're at it". I turned around to find Peter being held down while Tish, a wiry-thin, but tough girl, was hitting him. Peter, who in contrast is a tall, sturdy sixteen year old, suddenly broke free and started to punch her. I jumped on Peter and with an extraordinary strength that comes from terror, I pulled him away. Tish ran from the hall, shouting. For fear that she might leave the building before time, I ran after her, leaving a bunch of well revved-up teenagers on their own. I explained to her that I would be responsible if anything happened, etc..., but that she could wait elsewhere in the building until 3.30 p.m. — these events were occurring on a Wednesday afternoon when the entire warehouse was completely empty with not a single member of PACT present but myself...

Tish rushed back into the space ahead of me, yelling curses at Peter. I noticed that she picked something off the floor on her way in. She was taking aim about two feet away from Peter's cranium, when somehow I grabbed the brick doorstop from her hand. She then threatened to tell her father to "see to" and "deal with" Peter, all of which I could have ignored, but for the look of pure terror on Peter's face. They were obviously not empty threats.

There was a lull during which I was quietly shaking. I tried to make some 'meaningful' comments about how they had handled the power, and how the irresponsible use and exercise of power lead to violence. I mumbled on and no-one listened or understood.

After I calmed my nerves, I 'spilled the beans':

I explained that I did not enjoy the sessions at all; I was not being paid for doing them, and certainly did not intend to suffer out of the kindness of my heart. I could think of much better things to do with my time. I did not believe that they wanted to do drama sessions. If they liked coming here just to get off school for the afternoon, then they might as well go elsewhere because that space was in great demand for much more worthwhile things such as our own drama sessions and dance classes, rehearsals for performances and workshops with other outside groups. I could not think of a good reason for continuing the sessions with them.

There was a strong but quiet response. They said that they really wanted to "do" drama, and gave me examples of the things they particularly enjoyed. I softened and did not admit defeat.

The following lesson, I did not even pretend to be enthusiastic; asked them what they wanted to do; told them to get on and do it. By now they had a substantial stock of games and exercises from which to choose. Having gone through a number of them, they then requested some costumes and props in order to do an improvisation. The sessions after that became successively more enjoyable, less tiring. They seemed to organise themselves far more efficiently than I ever had.

At first the boys and girls worked in separate groups. As they needed members of the opposite sex in their stories, they mixed. They did not want me to give them a starting point but wanted to think up their own ideas. They called on me when they needed me. The only structure I imposed on the 'class' was that when they were ready, one group would sit and watch while the other performed and vice versa. We would conclude with a discussion of the pieces over a cup of tea.

The improvisations eventually became carefully constructed performances. They had learnt so much more from watching each other than any 'acting exercise' I had done with them. The quality of the discussions developed from rude and personal insults, to reasonably 'objective', perceptive comments. The most exciting experience of all, was to have seen the transformation of a particularly obstructive, seemingly lazy and inert teenager called Melanie, into a vital source of inspiration and director of ideas and actions in the performance pieces.

Most of them left school at the end of the spring term or beginning of the summer term.

AN EVENT

THE ONLY EXPERIENCE I had of the language of Rotherhithe entertainment, apart from the lunchtime striptease, was the 'Ship Show'.

The Ship was our local pub. Trixie, who lived opposite the Ship, was a regular customer and an active member of the immediate community. She had performed in 'The Business of

Good Government'. Since then she had remained a good friend of the students, mainly from her seat in the lounge bar.

She wanted to organize a benefit show in The Ship to raise money to provide local OAPs with a short holiday by the sea. She asked if we would help organize and perform in the show. She wanted it to be a 'Victorian Evening'. So we began planning ideas, like charging people who refused to have a moustache drawn on them. We made feather head-bands for the women. A local pearly king was contacted. And finally the group set about working on material for the show. Our quartet agreed to do their version of 'Yes Sir, That's my Baby'. Michael and myself started to rehearse a Wilson, Berry and Kepple routine called 'The Old Bazaar in Cairo'.

Two days before the show that was all we had. Our skills in the art of Rotherhithe entertainment were obviously limited. To fill in, the quartet did another of their songs 'On a Little Street in Singapore' combined with a visual joke I'd learnt using a third arm. Dave Slater did his escapology number, again.

We had arranged a stage in The Ship, which was in fact one 3 foot by 6 foot rostrum. During the performance of 'The Old Bazaar in Cairo', there were eight of us singing and dancing on it. Mike and I as a couple of bedouins and the girls as dancing harem maidens.

The start of the show was delayed until the pub was full and the stomachs were getting that way. The pearly king got it under-way and the first act was the quartet's first number. I gaffed my lines up in it but I don't think anyone heard, it was too noisy at the bar. The applause, however, was more than generous. While the next act, a flautist, did his thing, the group went off to get changed for the big number. When it came, things were warming up. The biggest laugh came when Jock, Trixie's husband, had his hands up Mike's and my nightshirts.

After that, performances became rather impromptu. We convinced Brian, a young member of RYPT, to get up and do something. We knew he would, we'd been plying him with cider all night. "You name it, I'll sing it!", he roared. Then he broke into the first two lines of 'Blue Suede Shoes', and "na na na' d" the rest of it. The pianist trying to accompany him couldn't believe it. Every time he caught up with what Brian was singing, Brian would stop, and then sing the first two lines of something else. He was dreadful and everybody loved it. Trixie then took to the microphone and started blasting out some of the old favourites. By now everybody was either joining in or having a go themselves.

It was an excellent evening's entertainment for all concerned. We collected over £100 in donations and auctions.

Royston Lambert (on right) with students in Conisbrough.

CHAPTER SEVEN

Some Concluding Thoughts

D ARTINGTON'S SIXTY YEARS of experiment with the idea of 'learning by doing' may be seen as a succession of attempts, some more successful than others, at breaking down the divisions that separate educational institutions from the world. What makes the projects described in this book particularly remarkable is that they have been set up in the context of the Dartington Hall Trust's multi-faceted range of activities, and against a background of a desire for a more integrated community.

Dartington, benefiting from small scale, and a unique spread of interests, has been able to take the idea of 'learning by doing' well beyond practical or vocational education. The Trust's experience since 1925, whether in pottery or horticultural training, work experience, or the training of community artists, suggests ways in which the acquisition of skills and knowledge might derive greater relevance and meaning — personally and socially — from being understood as part of a continuum of life experience, rather than as a specialised pursuit. Learning opportunities of this sort can, in the right circumstances, create a bridge between the maturing individual and the world, avoiding a dissociation between educational experience and our ordinary day to day reality (unlike most forms of education, which have cultivated this so assiduously since the Enlightenment).

In a rapidly changing culture, however, potential contradictions emerge in the apparently simple idea of 'learning by doing'. There is, on the one hand, an important trend in modern education which promotes a freedom gained through the development of detachment, objectivity, and the ability to question. The experimental method, which encourages a questioning attitude, practical testing of ideas, and adventures into the unknown, provides one of the major starting points for the contemporary understanding of 'learning by doing'. In contrast, the idea of 'learning by doing' is often understood in the context of the notion of practical apprenticeship — an initiation into traditional or accepted attitudes and practices. While the former approach is essentially radical and progressive, optimistically valuing reform or revolution, the latter is more conservative, with an emphasis on continuity and the inescapable and perennial 'facts of life' in a 'real' as opposed to a 'possible' or Utopian world.

Something of the tension between these two different interpretations of 'learning by doing' can be seen in a range of problems encountered at Dartington: in the early School, with the Estate as its classroom, the primacy given to the children's own wishes could not, in the long term, fit in with the everyday demands of forestry, gardens, poultry and other concerns. The desire of Pottery Training Workshop students to pursue their own personal ideas were in conflict with the commercial constraints of a business in which they were apprenticed employees as much as trainees. The Sicily Project, which transplanted highly individualistic former Foxhole students to a traditional rural setting collapsed, in part, because of a fundamental conflict of interests between the liberation promised by the sixties counter-culture and romantic aspirations towards an integrated back-to-nature existence. There is a great and perhaps unbridgeable distance, too, between the ideologically-derived practice to which students might aspire in the arts and the practical limitations of the fragmented communities in which they find themselves working during their year out or placement.

The same uncomfortable tension runs through Dartington's entire history — not just the Trust's ventures into education — for libertarian and progressive ideals do not mix easily with the idea of a reconstructed Estate in Devon. The pace, style and spirit of metropolitan and rural life are fundamentally different. Dartington, in trying to combine the best of two worlds, sets up an inevitable series of long-term misunderstandings: the Elmhirsts' aspirations, later taken up by the Trust, were predominantly experimental in outlook, whatever their content, while the peopled ground upon which they had chosen to work was suspicious of change and even more so of idealistic experimentation. Something of the same contradiction characterises the Romantic and Utopian traditions, and any other counter-cultural world view which espouses freedom and change, whilst at the same time, paradoxically, often being drawn nostalgically back to Eden and a lost wholeness or togetherness. The very idea of a counter-culture presupposes a restless dissatisfaction with the status quo, and is inevitably irreconcilable with the unquestioning stability of traditional life. There is a sense in which, once innocence has been lost to doubt and quest, there can be no turning back: the circle has been broken.

Two views of the world collide here in confusion: one perspective which looks forward and/or back, making comparative evaluations as it does so, and another which focuses upon the continuities in which concepts of past, present and future shrink into relative insignificance. The former view is coloured by the lure of future possibility, and, correspondingly, often carries within it the sense of a forsaken natural state characterised by wholeness and perfection, however these might be defined. Whether history is viewed as a progression forwards and upwards from poverty, ignorance and inhumanity, or as a recovery of a state before the 'Fall' is, in this context, not so important: both perspectives are in an essential sense historical. They depend upon a linear view of time, in which one stage of a progression follows another and moves towards a better or less ideal world. The second way of understanding time, however, is concerned more with recurring cycles, continuity and repetition; it is more important within such a belief system to find one's place.

Within the Utopian tradition, the historical and traditional views have become so entangled that it is at times difficult to distinguish between them. There is, as it were, a desire to opt

149

out of history, to return to a stable pre-historical world, but this wish remains trapped, in most instances, within a resolutely linear expectation of ever-increasing potential.

In superimposing a 'school for adventure' and an experimental outlook on the conservative cultural landscape of Devon, the Elmhirsts could not avoid facing the contradictions inherent in the notion of revitalisation of the countryside, and the inevitable friction between two very different outlooks and rhythms of existence. The city, which is characterised by constant movement and change, demands an education which facilitates mobility, a learning by doing that allows for independence, self-sufficiency and adaptability, and leads outwards and forwards. The countryside, at least traditionally and in its romantic presentation, demands a different kind of adaptation: it requires an acceptance of structures and relationships as they exist, as well as an initiation into conventions, rituals and place. Contemporary Britain, of course, offers very little in the way of such a pure rural context: the inroads made by the mass media and mobility — geographical as well as social — have greatly reduced the powerful sense of order that comes from 'knowing one's place'. Yet something undoubtedly remains — and not just in the fantasies of unhappy city-dwellers.

Drawn towards an image of place, culture, knowledge reintegrated, Dartington has been caught between two myths: the myth of science, experiment and progress on the one hand, and the more conservative myth of integration or wholeness on the other. Each of these myths suggests a different application of the idea of learning by doing: one that favours individual freedom and experiential exploration, and the other that places a value on apprenticeship, continuity and the collective experience. In attempting to provide the best of urban and rural life, it is clear that the Elmhirsts wished to provide for a community that would allow for a balance between stability and change, individuality and co-operation.

At their best, Dartington's ventures into learning by doing suggest that the attempt to structure an educational experience which achieves some sort of balance between these opposing concerns, however difficult, may be worth undertaking, even though these represent only tentative beginnings in terms of Tagore's vision of a reintegrated community. For all the attraction of a reintegrated 'full life', there is, however, a deep and understandable resistance to the degree of stability and rootedness necessary to support such an existence: it is less exciting, mobile and free, and there are some good reasons for the high value which our culture places on expanding horizons.

At Dartington, 'place' has played a crucial part in encouraging the idea of an integrated community: the medieval buildings, the gardens, and the strong atmosphere of the fields and woodlands encircled by a wide bend in the river Dart, all contribute to a magic that draws people with the promise of an irresistible potential for nurturing a sense of wholeness. This promise, however, is only ever partially fulfilled, and the Trust's history presents a succession of thwarted attempts at making links across the boundaries that seem to stand in the way of a more integrated Estate.

It should be clear by now, however, that 'integration', the 'full-life' or the 'breaking down of specialisms and institutional boundaries' provide valuable images, ideas or models rather than goals that can be concretely achieved: they suggest 'frames of mind', and what Dartington might offer is a good context for this sort of 're-framing'.

One of Dartington's strongest distinguishing features (as well as many of its difficulties) arises out of its special position between city and country: between mobility and rootedness in place; and between change and continuity. Dartington's experience of learning by doing has reflected a corresponding polarity — in this case between learning as inquiry or experiment and learning as apprenticeship. Depending on your point of view, Dartington is either torn apart by ambivalence, or creatively brings together polar opposites. I am, personally, inclined to suggest that both perspectives are equally valid and need to be held in the mind's eye simultaneously: a sense of wholeness which can encompass such opposites, though deeply uncomfortable, can also be rich and rewarding.

The Elmhirsts' great wealth enabled the adventure to be launched, but inevitably created a distance between visionary enablers and the projects which were set up. That enabling space has been taken over by the Trustees, who carry out their Trusteeship with a necessary detachment and great responsibility, but with the protection afforded by only an indirect involvement in the business of survival. Yet a real sense of an integrated community is only likely to arise out of a shared struggle for survival, rather than in the protected context of a 'seedbed for new ideas'. And it would seem that Dartington's grant-making resources tend, more than anything, to encourage rivalry on the Estate as they tend to favour the creation of new projects.

There would be no Dartington without the detachment that enables experiment, but in terms of re-creating a sense of circle, of community — of seeing the whole rather than the parts — there is the inescapable fact that the Trust's degree of detachment holds the circle open and tends to keep all of Dartington's ventures as experiments, which are launched or facilitated by the Trust and then remain in constant need of 'parental' support. There is no easy answer to this question, and it is perhaps, in Dartington's rich and contradictory context, unanswerable. There is a need to keep the contradictions in the foreground of awareness, and to work with them, rather than against them.

In terms of the theme of learning by doing, this would suggest that Dartington can, at the very least, offer a context in which the ideas of apprenticeship and individual inquiry, initiation into the known and given, and the discovery of a personal perspective, might be balanced. This would give the idea of integration yet another meaning, for it would involve, as well as a mix of educational styles, an equilibrium between intellect, feeling, imagination and manual or practical work. Such an education would, above all, begin from a sense of place, the ground of the Estate and the traditions of our culture, as well as a point in moving time, and an opening towards change.

Students on Dartington's Forestry Training course in the 1970s.

Practical Training on the Estate

FORESTRY AND HORTICULTURE

THE SETTING UP of Dartington Hall Limited as the holding company for 'commercial' activities on the Estate, in 1929, and the establishment of the Trust in 1931, were both reflections of radical retrenchment. Along with the School's development as a separate institution in the 1930s, and the appointment of W. B. Curry as its head, these moves reflected a shift towards formalisation and the creation of separate communities at Dartington — groups within the Estate which 'spoke different languages' and held different values.

The Elmhirsts remained committed, however, to the idea that the Estate could provide a place in which learning was central to all activities, of both adults and children. Each of the commercial ventures — whether cider-making, 'economic' dairy farming, cattle breeding, forestry, or textiles — was to be experimental, and its progress monitored. These experiments were all intended to provide models for the rest of the world at a time when the government as yet only sponsored practical research to a very limited extent.

Adult education has also always played an important role on the Estate, with a wide range of artists, craftsmen, musicians and dancers offering invaluable opportunities for learning outside the conventional boundaries of a school, college or university. Dartington had not achieved the ideal community which Leonard and Dorothy may have dreamed of in 1925, but it was none the less unique for the way in which it gathered together such a range of activities and people. Dartington has remained, for over 60 years, a learning community.

There has been a sustained commitment, rooted in the founders' original vision, to provide opportunities, too, for specifically vocational training on the Estate. All of these have been highly practical, and designed to offer a non-institutional setting for the development of a number of skills.

FORESTRY

A S EARLY AS THE 1930s a number of courses were offered by the pioneering Woodlands Department. Stuart Bunce, who worked as as forester at Dartington during the war years and set up a training course for woodmen at Dartington in 1944, was appointed by the Trustees in 1966 to set up a Forestry Workers' Training Scheme. At the outset, the Trustees fully supported the Scheme; later there was some help from public sources, through government training boards. The considerable initial support from the Trust reflected in particular Leonard Elmhirst's own passion for forestry, as well as his conviction that learning was best done by doing. "Degrees in forestry in the UK can still be won by those who have never yet worked for a 12-month cycle in the woods", Leonard wrote in a 1974 booklet.

The training was to be based in Dartington's own commercial woodlands, combining two years of practical experience with further classroom education. The Forestry Training Centre was designed to fill an existing gap in forestry training and was specifically intended for Secondary Modern school-leavers without qualifications, who wished to train as forestry workers. As with other later training courses for school-leavers at Dartington, there was also a strong emphasis on facilitating the transition from school and home life into the adult world, and the trainees were encouraged to start taking responsibility for themselves. The trainees were paid wages and the combination of earning and learning gave a strong feeling of genuine work.

The commercial setting of the Forestry Training Centre made this project unique and Stuart Bunce was very much aware of the problems raised by the combination of training and financial objectives, particularly as regards the relationship between practical work and lecture courses: "The practical training in the forest should all the time be closely complementary to the lecture room periods, in that order. This can be a very difficult system to arrange as the commercial demands vary from day to day. Sometimes it is impossible to follow up a lecture with the practical application or aspect of the subject. For example, it would be ideal to lecture on the theory of thinning and then follow it up with a practical demonstration in the forest — but an order for plants from the nurseries might have to take priority and so upset any neat and tidy arrangement."

As can be seen from Stuart Bunce's booklet, *Training the Young Forester* (1974), the course was highly sensitive to the trainee's needs and sympathetic to the particular problems facing youngsters in the difficult transition from school to work. Institutional training tends to reinforce the dependence on authority which is characteristic of home life. Training at Dartington — with its setting in the adult world — allowed the trainees to start taking responsibility for themselves. The use of continuous assessment rather than end-of-year examinations (a method of assessment much closer to the conditions under which success or failure are established in the world beyond educational institutions) also distinguished Dartington training from more institutionalised courses.

In 1976 the Forestry Training Centre was closed down, mainly because it was no longer receiving support from public sources and the Dartington Hall Trustees were unwilling to wholly back each student's training. The Trustees' commitment to forestry had also declined. This was not surprising as the woodlands had been a personal passion of Leonard Elmhirst, and he had gradually withdrawn from Trust affairs during the 1960s and died in 1974. Most of the Trust-owned woodlands had been managed by Fountain Forestry since 1967, with the home woods coming under their care just over a decade later.

The Trust no longer owns the entire acreage of woods originally bought by the Elmhirsts. Only the home woods remain wholly Dartington's. In spite of this, in 1986 the Dartington

157

Institute launched a new forestry venture, Project Sylvanus, which included the establishment of the Dartington Centre for Woodland Training, based at the Old Postern and later brought under the aegis of the Dartington Tech as the Dartington Forestry Training Group. The Group offers short-term training courses for youngsters and adults in a number of craft and woodland skills, but has little in common with the earlier wide-ranging residential courses offered to school-leavers.

HORTICULTURE

I N 1950 the Dartington Hall Trust set up a horticultural training scheme for 'boys direct from Devon schools'. The Scheme was run — as several other Dartington educational ventures — with Devon County Council. Each year, two bursaries were made available, for one to three years. These scholarships were residential. The training was both practical and theoreti-cal, and the youngsters were expected to do a number of external courses as well. By the mid 1960s the course had become known as the Grounds and Gardens Training Scheme, and later as the Horticultural Training Centre, which offered training to male and female school-leavers in a wide range of theoretical and practical skills. Unlike other courses, Dartington's was not specialist in content. Students were accommodated in the Gardens Hostel on the Estate and were paid basic wages. The students were also expected to take a number of key exams including a Royal Horticultural Society exam, the Dartington Hall Garden Diploma, City and Guilds Stage 1, and also various 'O' levels, where necessary. The Scheme continued to be supported by the county, but now also received support from Local Education Authorities from all over Britain as it became open to students from outside Devon. Out of a 42-hour week, trainees spent a maximum of 21 hours on practical work, and a minimum of 12 hours on lectures. There was some involvement with other parts of the Estate, especially the School, which offered 'O' level tuition for the trainees.

As with the parallel Forestry Training Centre, the horticultural course stressed the importance of the transition from the sheltered atmosphere of school to the world of work. Most of the students lived in at the hostel or at the Postern, which was at that time used by the school's sixth form section.

In 1976 the Training Centre was closed down, mainly because crucial government funds had been gradually withdrawn. With the development of the MSC, however, and a growing sense in government circles of the need to find ways of tackling the unemployment of school-leavers, a new horticultural training scheme was set up in 1980. Dartington's Horticultural Training Workshop ran as a six-month course until July 1982, when it was expanded to cover a full year. The object of the workshop was "to give specialist training in considerable depth to young people of a varied range of abilities, from non-academic to those wishing to go on to College and University". The year's training consisted of two terms based at Dartington and two more three-month periods on placement with horticultural employers. From April 1983, the workshop was granted the status of a 'Mode B' course under the government's new Youth Training Scheme. In line with other YTS projects the Horticultural Training Workshop also offered some training in 'life and social skills', but this was a pale though not entirely insignificant version of the programmes that were so central to Dartington's Work Experience and Postern Programmes. In most years there have been 32 trainees, and the Workshop has generally been regarded as a success. The training period lasts, at the time of writing, six months.

ROYSTON LAMBERT'S ATTEMPTS, in the late 1960s, to integrate the forestry and horticultural workshops with the School were not successful. However, the perseverance with which the Trust has backed practical training schemes over the years, and continues to do so, reflects a real commitment. The fact that such projects have always been conducted in almost water-tight compartments, not easily integrating with other activities on the Estate, has had more to do with Dartington's history and long-standing cultural habits than with the short-comings of individual human beings. This 'failing' — at least in terms of a vision that looks towards maximum integration rather than specialisation — is probably also largely due to inescapable differences between the expectations of various groups. For example, Dartington Hall School parents were on the whole concerned for their children to gather qualifications, whereas the parents of unemployed school-leavers had other interests at heart, as the meagre qualifications of these youngsters were likely to open no doors for them at all.

The wish for integration, here as with other Dartington projects, was confronted in practice with a web of entrenched preferences and habitual ways of perceiving the value of education. Alongside an increasingly pessimistic view of the school-leaver's opportunities there was, from the early 1980s, a general cultural shift, which inevitably affected Dartington, away from the common interests associated with visions of reintegration and towards a more 'realistic', pragmatic and competitive ethos. In this new formulation, education's primary role became the enhancement of work or career prospects, and many of the earlier values were inevitably left behind.

The Great Hall, Dartington.